MOON

52 THINGS TO DO IN

CHICAGO

ROSALIND CUMMINGS-YEATES

CONTENTS

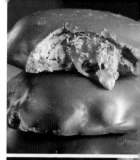

Day Trips and Getaways

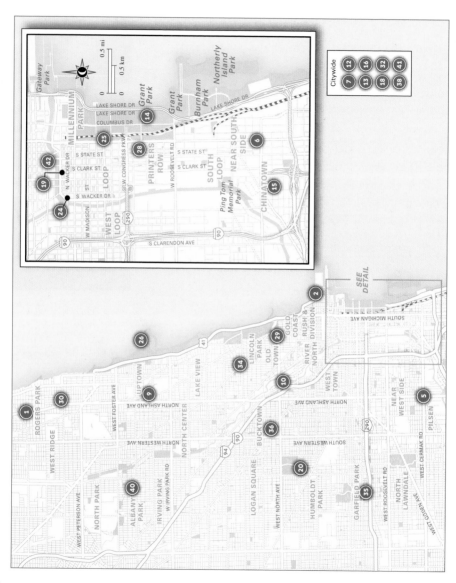

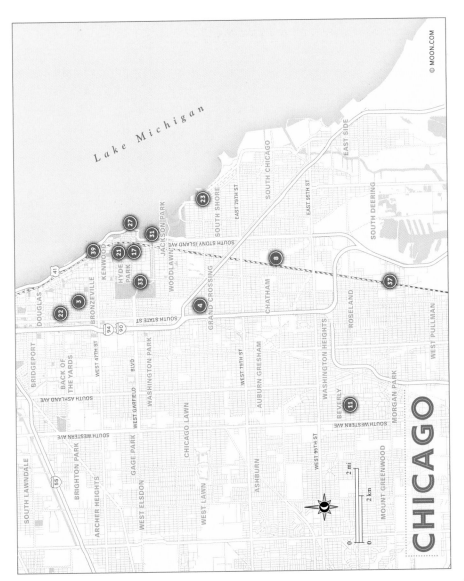

CHICAGO

Lake Michigan

© MOON.COM

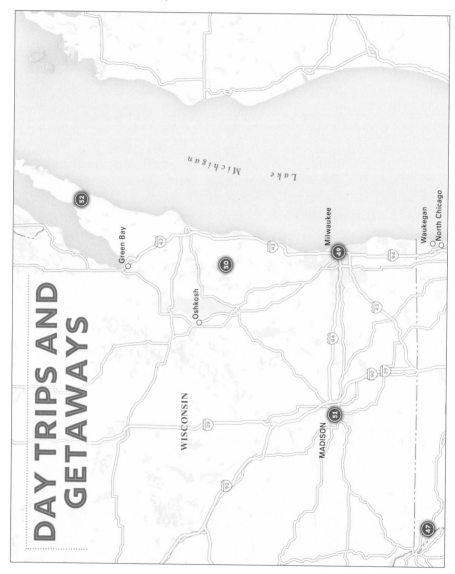

DAY TRIPS AND GETAWAYS

WISCONSIN

Green Bay

Oshkosh

Milwaukee

MADISON

Waukegan
North Chicago

Lake Michigan

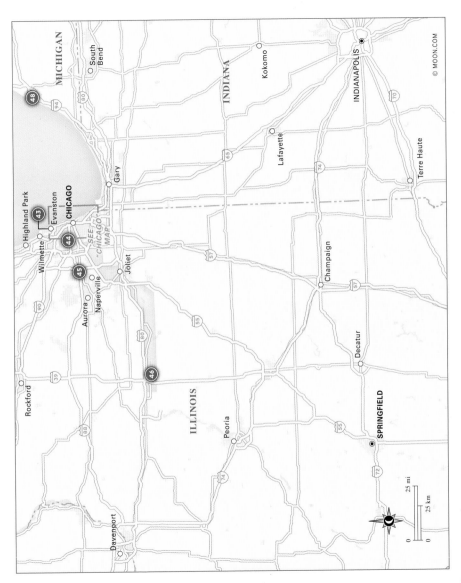

© MOON.COM

9

THIS IS MY CHICAGO

The streets of Chicago crackle with energy and history. Vibrant personalities, softened by Midwestern warmth, flow through its 77 neighborhoods. Chicago isn't showy like L.A. or worldly like New York; it's a big city wrapped in small-town sensibilities, both grounded and passionate. Living here grants you hustle and heart. Though this is a place where people still say hello when walking down the street, it requires real contact and honest effort to connect with the essence of Chi-Town. But if you spend some time interacting with locals and picking up the lingo, you will be rewarded.

I grew up on a placid South Side street, lined with wide lawns and laughter, called Avalon. It was here that I learned essential Chicago lifestyle standards: how to get the best seat on the "L" (shorthand for "elevated train"), how to represent the city's best baseball team (go White Sox!), and how to glide across the floor in the Steppin' dance (a quintessential Chi-Town dance that has had couples swaying since the '50s). Since then, I've lived all over the city, from Chatham, to Lakeview, to Rogers Park.

What I love about my city is that each neighborhood is like its own little village, with its own rules, main squares, and even unofficial mayors. While Chicago is famed for the glossy architecture of the Loop and the bikes, beers, and Cubs flags of the North Side, its lesser-known neighborhoods are where its spirit really shines. There's Pilsen, where Mexican heritage and street art create a warm community; Hyde Park, where the city's love of arts and culture takes center stage; and Rogers Park, where the raw energy of a diverse population lends a free-wheeling open-mindedness.

This is my Chicago and I'd love to take you there.

Chicago Riverwalk

TO DO LISTS

Chi-Town Essential

4 Savor **South Side barbecue**

6 Groove to the **Chicago blues**

8 **Roller-skate** Chicago style

13 Listen to classic **Chicago jazz**

14 Get out to **Grant Park**

18 Chow down on **classic Chicago eats**

22 Get inspired by Black art at the **South Side Community Art Center**

23 Take a trip down **LSD**

24 Ramble the **Riverwalk**

25 See world-class Impressionist art at the **Art Institute of Chicago**

29 Laugh out loud at **Second City**

37 Learn about labor history at the **Pullman National Monument**

Food and Drink

1 Wander the world in **Rogers Park**

4 Savor **South Side barbecue**

7 Drink in local flavor at **neighborhood cafés**

12 Feast on **Senegalese cuisine**

15 Enjoy the cultural feast of **Chinatown**

18 Chow down on **classic Chicago Eats**

21 Eat your way down **53rd Street**

32 Scoop up **sweet treats**

35 Enjoy greens with a side of **soul food** in Garfield Park

41 Taste sweet **candy history**

49 Indulge in **brats and brews** in Milwaukee, Wisconsin

51 **Dine lakeside** in Madison, Wisconsin

Wall of Honor project by students of Solorio High School and the J-DEF Peace Project

Arts and Culture

3 Go **gallery-hopping** in Bronzeville

5 Stroll the **street art** in Pilsen

6 Groove to the **Chicago blues**

9 Celebrate music and history at **Black Ensemble Theater**

13 Listen to classic **Chicago jazz**

16 Browse **community bookstores**

20 Celebrate Borinquén culture at the
National Museum of Puerto Rican Arts & Culture

22 Get inspired by Black art at the **South Side Community Art Center**

25 See world-class Impressionist art at the **Art Institute of Chicago**

28 Wander the urban canvas at the **Wabash Arts Corridor**

29 Laugh out loud at **Second City**

34 See a play (or two) at the historic **Biograph Theater**

38 Tune in to **live local music**

40 Appreciate Indigenous culture at the **American Indian Center**

Get Outside

② Bike the **Lakefront Trail**

⑩ **Kayak** the Chicago River

⑭ Get out to **Grant Park**

⑲ Hop a **water taxi** from the Loop

㉔ Ramble the **Riverwalk**

㉖ Paddle and play in the water at **Montrose Beach**

㉗ Catch the views from **Promontory Point**

㉛ Find peace at **Garden of the Phoenix**

㊱ Amble along the elevated **606** trail

㊴ Explore the **Burnham Wildlife Corridor**

㊸ Walk in the woods at **Morton Arboretum**

㊻ Hike in **Starved Rock State Park**

㊽ **Hit the beach in St. Joseph,** Michigan

㊿ Relax at **Elkhart Lake,** Wisconsin

㊾ Enjoy the bounty of **Door County,** Wisconsin

Black Chicago

3 Go gallery-hopping in **Bronzeville**

4 Savor **South Side barbecue**

6 Groove to the **Chicago blues**

8 **Roller-skate** Chicago style

9 Celebrate music and history at **Black Ensemble Theater**

12 Feast on **Senegalese cuisine**

21 Eat your way down **53rd Street**

22 Get inspired by Black art at the **South Side Community Art Center**

33 Appreciate Chicago's Black roots at the
DuSable Museum of African American History

37 Learn about labor history at the **Pullman National Monument**

From Bloom to Doom by Collin van der Sluijs

Neighborhoods and City Streets

Family Fun

⑨ Celebrate music and history at **Black Ensemble Theater**

⑭ Get out to **Grant Park**

㉖ Paddle and play in the water at **Montrose Beach**

㉜ Scoop up **sweet treats**

㉟ Enjoy greens with a side of soul food in **Garfield Park**

㊱ Amble along the elevated **606** trail

㊶ Taste sweet **candy history**

㊺ Walk in the woods at **Morton Arboretum**

㊽ Hit the beach in **St. Joseph,** Michigan

㊿ Relax at **Elkhart Lake,** Wisconsin

Get Out of Town

43 Explore the eclectic in **Evanston**

44 Retrace Hemingway's footsteps in **Oak Park**

45 Walk in the woods at **Morton Arboretum**

46 Hike in **Starved Rock State Park**

47 Go back in time in **Galena,** Illinois

48 Hit the beach in **St. Joseph,** Michigan

49 Indulge in brats and brews in **Milwaukee,** Wisconsin

50 Relax at **Elkhart Lake,** Wisconsin

51 Dine lakeside in **Madison,** Wisconsin

52 Enjoy the bounty of **Door County,** Wisconsin

1 Wander the world in Rogers Park

Neighborhoods and City Streets • Food and Drink • Arts and Culture

Why Go: Feel like you're in another country without buying a plane ticket by visiting Chicago's most diverse neighborhood.

Where: Neighborhood roughly bordered by Howard St. in the north and Devon Ave. in the south, extending east from Ridge Blvd. to Lake Michigan • L train Red Line to Howard (northern end) or Loyola (southern end)

Timing: An afternoon in Rogers Park gives you time to sample its many flavors, including a mix of international fare (come hungry!), street art, and shops.

Language is the music that floats through Rogers Park. Other neighborhoods might have hip-hop or salsa booming from windows, but in Rogers Park, it's the lilt of Gujarati, the punch of Polish, or the rhythm of Yoruba that form the area's soundtrack. Perched on Lake Michigan, this is a beachfront community with an artsy, gritty vibe. Some consider this a college neighborhood since Loyola University dominates a major portion along **Sheridan Road,** where you'll see students milling around the Starbucks and Loyola Beach and Park. But this is also a place of immigrant dreams, of tree-lined streets and green landscapes, of ramshackle shops and indie theaters. Elegant courtyard buildings, sprawling 19th-century homes, and high-rise apartments might all share space on a single block. As the northernmost neighborhood in Chicago, Rogers Park is often overlooked; frankly, it's a hike to get here—almost 10 miles from the Loop—but its under-the-radar treasures make it the perfect place for itchy-foot culture lovers.

The first time I stepped into Rogers Park was to visit an underground Ethiopian restaurant in someone's apartment (my friend knew the owner). I remember the thrill of eating fresh injera and lentil stew while sitting in an easy chair. After sipping *tej,* a heady honey wine, I strolled out onto a bustling sidewalk filled with people selling jewelry and incense. Arabic music blared, and the smell of roasting *elote* (grilled Mexican street corn) filled the air. There was an atmosphere of surprise around every corner and colorful revelry, similar to the sensation you might get at open-air markets in Latin America or the Caribbean. I remember thinking,

▲ *Resilience* mural by artist Gretchen Hasse

▲ Lady B Boutique

"How come I've never visited this cool neighborhood?" I now live in Rogers Park, and those initial feelings of enchantment I first experienced decades ago still surge through me every time I stroll through my eclectic surroundings.

Rogers Park used to be the land of the Potawatomi, Chippewa, and Ottawa people. **Indian Boundary Park** (2500 W. Lunt St.), just west of the neighborhood's borders proper, is an oasis and reminder of the area's original residents, who were driven out by various treaties in the early 19th century. By the early 20th century, wealthy business owners lived in Rogers Park—until WWI, when waves of immigrants from Eastern Europe, Italy, Ireland, and Russia arrived. From then on, each decade brought new groups of immigrants, hailing from regions including Southeast Asia, Africa, the Caribbean, and the Middle East, creating the global mix that the neighborhood is noted for.

Start your exploration of Rogers Park at **Howard Street,** the boundary between Chicago and Evanston, and terminus of the L's Red Line. You'll glimpse lots of activity in front of the station, from vendors selling cell phone plans to evangelists peddling saved souls. A walk east from the L past a wig store and a leafy community garden brings you to the **Caribbean American Bakery** (1539 W. Howard St., 773/761-0700, www.caribbeanamericanbakery.com), a community outpost. The smell of Jamaican hard dough bread baking floats through the air, and on weekends, locals line up for the bakery's jerk chicken dinners. But most people come for the patties—savory pastries filled with seasoned beef, curried chicken, spinach, or vegetables. If there's a wait, pop into **Lady B Boutique** (1547 W. Howard St., 312/714-2485), a couple of doors down, where you can browse an assortment of vibrant island-style dresses, shirts, and shorts while grooving to a reggae soundtrack.

Make your way south on **Clark Street,** one of the neighborhood's primary thoroughfares. It's lined with cafés, shops, taquerias, *panaderías* (bakeries), and even a quinceañera boutique. Stop at **Taste of Peru** (6545 N. Clark St., 773/381-4540, http://tasteofperu.com) to try delicacies like fried yuca with cheese sauce or Peruvian-style tamales, and wash them down with *chicha morada,* a tasty purple corn drink. Or try some injera for yourself at the nearby **Denden Restaurant** (6635 N. Clark St., 773/973-4752), a family-owned diner that's the city's only Eritrean eatery.

East of and parallel to Clark Street is **Glenwood Avenue.** Head here to view the **Mile of**

Murals (http://mileofmurals.com/home.html), along the L's Red Line track between Estes and Pratt. The community-based initiative features the faces and symbols of Chicago's most diverse neighborhood as interpreted by a range of artists, including beginners, art students and teachers, art collectives, and well-known local artists like Hebru Brantley. You'll spot murals of rainbow-colored bikers representing the open-mindedness and active nature of the community; local leaders like Charlotte Goldberg and Tobey Prinz, both of whom fought against high-rises and worked to preserve public beach access; and Barack Obama—gazing off into the distance with circles of red and white framing his head like a halo—who kicked off his senate campaign at a former Rogers Park community anchor, the now-shuttered Heartland Cafe.

Heading south on either Clark Street or Glenwood Avenue, you'll eventually arrive at **Devon Avenue,** the neighborhood's southern border. Head west past Ridge Boulevard into the adjacent neighborhood of **West Ridge,** also called **West Rogers Park.** Just strolling down this street, nicknamed **Little India** for its plethora of Indian stores and eateries, is transporting, with Bollywood tunes streaming out of shops and glistening displays of sarees and gold jewelry in every other window. Drop by **Sona Chandi Boutique** (2659 W. Devon Ave., 773/262-6787) for well-priced *salwar kameez* (traditional tunic and trouser sets) or **Shop N' Help** (6377 N. California Ave., 773/819-9233), a community nonprofit offering handmade purses, jewelry, and kitchen goods. Top off your journey with a visit to **Sukhadia** (2559 W. Devon Ave., 773/338-5400, www.sukhadiasweetschicago.com), an Indian candy shop with flavors like chickpea, cardamom, and carrot.

Connect with . . .

30 Learn about leather at the Leather Archives & Museum

2 Bike the Lakefront Trail

Why Go: Actively appreciate the splendor of Chicago's crown jewel on a two-wheeled shoreline ride.

Where: Along Lake Michigan from Ardmore Ave. in the north to E. 71st St. in the south • www.chicagoparkdistrict.com • L train Red Line to Thorndale (northern trailhead) or Grand (Ohio Street Beach)

Timing: Bicyclists can ride the entire 18-mile trail (one-way) in about 1.75 hours without stops, though crowds will likely slow your pace. This recommended route is roughly 8 miles one-way, just under an hour's ride, but give yourself a half day to explore. Many pedestrians hop on and off the trail as they like.

Striking landmarks cap off Chicago's skyline, but nothing defines the city's landscape more than Lake Michigan, and nothing is more beloved by Chicagoans. Sure, we adore our pizza and sports, but the lake is the pride of the entire city. No matter what political or economic turmoil pops up to bother us, just gazing at the blue waves lapping the coastline brings joy and peace, even knocking off some of the pain of the seemingly endless winter months. One of the best ways to appreciate the lake's breadth and diverse offerings is to bike or walk the Lakefront Trail, which links many of the city's neighborhoods, parks, beaches, and attractions.

Summer is peak season, when the roughly 18-mile Lakefront Trail is thronged with an average of 30,000 walkers, joggers, bikers, skaters, e-scooters, wheelchair users, and more daily. Fortunately, in 2018 the trail was separated into parallel two-way biking and walking paths, which eases the congestion. The trail is mostly flat and paved for easy traction. Go midmorning or midweek to avoid the biggest crowds in summer. I prefer to head out on the trail in fall, when the trees lining the path turn gold and red, and people are fewer and farther between. Although the Lakefront Trail is accessible year-round, the winds and waves licking at the edges of the path can be vicious in winter.

My favorite parts of the trail are along its southern half, and I love gliding down the paved

Divvy bike rental

Lakefront Trail

cyclists on the lakeshore

pathway on my bike; it's much easier to maneuver through the throngs on two wheels. **Divvy bike rentals** (www.divvybikes.com, $15 day pass) are available via the city's bicycle-sharing program at convenient spots along the Lakefront Trail, including the starting and ending points described here.

Start at tiny **Ohio Street Beach** (E. Ohio St. and N. Lake Shore Dr.), a pocket of sand tucked just northwest of **Navy Pier**'s tourist bustle. While the trail runs through lots of beaches, this one is more secluded, has lovely skyline views, and is home to **Caffè Oliva** (550 E. Grand Ave. 312/612-0734, www.caffeoliva.com, Memorial Day weekend-Sept.), known for offering "sustenance on the sand"; situated right on the beach and surrounded by a small park, it's a scenic setting in which to fuel up for your ride. My go-tos are the fish tacos and parmesan truffle fries. The café also supplies a restroom, which is a big deal as there are only a handful scattered along the trail in park field houses and beaches.

Head south from here to begin rolling through the leafy scenery of **Grant Park** and past the landmark Beaux-Arts beauty of the **Buckingham Fountain** and the **Museum Campus**.

▲ Chicago skyline

It's especially fun to ride by **Soldier Field,** with its distinctive, neoclassical colonnades and expanse of parking lots; the stadium is like its own contained village. Soon after passing it, you'll ride through **Burnham Park,** and on the horizon see long lines of boats bobbing at **31st Street Harbor.**

That's my signal that I'll soon need to turn briefly off the trail at the 47th Street Bridge to ride through the **Burnham Nature Sanctuary,** part of the **Burnham Wildlife Corridor.** Bicyclists are allowed to ride through the sanctuary, which hosts different habitats and numerous birds. I like to follow the paved path (veer left upon entering) that connects to the boardwalk, which runs through grassland and a butterfly garden, and pause to watch the colorful insects flutter around wildflowers and native shrubs.

I tend to get so taken with the scenery in the sanctuary that I rarely ride much farther. But it's worth it to make the extra effort and hop back on the Lakefront Trail. Pedal another mile and a half south to reach a sublime end goal: **Promontory Point** (at 55th St.), a parkland offering the most rewarding panoramas in the city.

Connect with . . .

⓮ Get out to Grant Park
㉗ Catch the views from Promontory Point
㊴ Explore the Burnham Wildlife Corridor

3 Go gallery-hopping in Bronzeville

Black Chicago • Arts and Culture • Neighborhoods and City Streets

Why Go: View contemporary exhibits of Black art in a historic African American neighborhood.

Where: Neighborhood roughly bordered by 31st St. in the north and 47th St. in the south, extending east from I-90 to Cottage Grove Ave. • L train Green Line to 35th-Bronzeville-IIT, Indiana, 43rd, or 47th

Timing: You can enjoy a few hours of gallery-hopping year-round, but one of the best times to visit is on the third Friday of the month July-October, when a seasonal trolley tour runs between galleries and special opening parties are held.

Bronzeville's streets vibrate with echoes of history and culture. In the exodus between 1916 and 1970 known as the Great Migration, more than six million African Americans relocated to northern cities from the Jim Crow South, and this neighborhood, along with Harlem in New York, became a beacon for Black creativity and enterprise, earning the nickname the "Black Metropolis." Signature strains of blues, gospel, and jazz, as well as fine art and literature, were nurtured here. Gwendolyn Brooks and Lorraine Hansberry created literary classics, and Nat King Cole and Louis Armstrong established their musical genius here. This was also the neighborhood where Daniel Hale Williams, an African American cardiologist, completed the world's first open-heart surgery. Today, the Bronzeville art scene is still thriving, and three vibrant Black-owned galleries offer great insight into it.

Known for its exciting displays of work from across the African diaspora, **Gallery Guichard** (436 E. 47th St., 773/791-7003, www.galleryguichard.com) is the premier Bronzeville art gallery. Sleek and well-curated, the gallery throws openings that feel like sophisticated house parties. One of my favorites showcased sculptures, paintings, and mixed media pieces by local as well as international artists, including some powerful displays about the Black experience across borders. It was a warm September evening, and the gallery's sculpture garden was decked out with chairs and a DJ. A bar served drinks, and table of hors d'oeuvres provided

Gallery Guichard

Blanc Gallery

fortification. Artist studios were also open on the building's 2nd floor, so you could pop into the small spaces and watch artists at work and talk with them about their pieces as jazz floated in the background.

For thought-provoking, multidisciplinary works that incorporate film and music, **Blanc Gallery** (4445 S. Martin Luther King Dr., 773/373-4320, www.blancchicago.com) is your place. The stark white space hosts art intended to stimulate community discussions around political and social issues. One notable work featured the riveting spectacle of laughing kids, images of body parts, and vintage TV commercials mixed together into a montage video that left me unsettled. My feelings were addressed during a lively panel discussion between artists and activists that probed the ways such imagery affects how Black women are treated in the U.S.

Faie Afrikan Art (1005 E. 43rd St.,773/268-2889, http://faieafrikanart.com) is an intimate space that showcases art from West, Central, Eastern, and Southern Africa, particularly functional pieces that have been used for spiritual connection, sacred adornment, and traditional ceremonies. The eclectic array includes carved masks, heavy coral necklaces, handmade

Faie Afrikan Art

More to Explore in Historic Bronzeville

Check out more of Bronzeville's legacy by visiting historic landmarks including Civil Rights activist and journalist **Ida B. Wells-Barnett's greystone mansion** (3624 S. King Dr.) and the building that from 1920-1960 housed the country's first nationally circulated African American newspaper, the ***Chicago Defender*** (3445 S. Indiana Ave.). Wander the **Bronzeville Walk of Fame** (S. Martin Luther King Dr. between E. 25th St. and E. 35th St.), which features 91 bronze plaques honoring famous former neighborhood residents like aviator Bessie Coleman, singer Sam Cooke, and choreographer and dancer Katherine Dunham. And don't miss the ***Monument to the Great Northern Migration*** (S. Martin Luther King Dr. and 26th St.), featuring a towering bronze man holding a suitcase and oriented north in honor of the people who fled their Southern homes and settled here to create the Bronzeville community.

dolls, and feathered headdresses. Presided over by vivacious owner Faye Edwards, the inviting gallery hosts artist talks and festive openings with live music in the basement.

One of the best ways to visit the galleries is to hop on the **Bronzeville Art District Trolley Tour** (www.bronzevilleartdistrict.com, 6pm-9pm every third Fri. July-Oct., free). It stops at these galleries and others, all of which host openings with snacks and maybe some drinks, plus activities like live music performances and artist discussions. I usually stop beforehand at **Some Like It Black Creative Arts Bar** (810 E. 43rd St., 773/891-4866, www.somelikeitblack.com) for an almond joy smoothie and turkey taco. The tiny space also hosts artwork, poetry readings, live music, and DJ sets.

Connect with . . .

4 Savor South Side barbecue (Honey 1 BBQ)

12 Feast on Senegalese cuisine (Yassa African Restaurant, Gorée Cuisine)

22 Get inspired by Black art at the South Side Community Art Center

Savor South Side barbecue

Chi-Town Essential • Food and Drink • Black Chicago

Why Go: Try a Chicago food staple that dates back to the 1930s and transcends the trends.

Where: The South Side boasts lots of barbecue joints, with many of the traditional ones concentrated in the Bronzeville, Chatham, and South Shore neighborhoods.

Timing: These are all carry-out joints, so you can budget less than an hour for each. Menu items can sell out, so on weekends—which which tend to be busier—the earlier you arrive, the better.

Chicago is famous for many culinary contributions, but barbecue isn't typically one of them. Yet historians date the first South Side barbecue joint to the 1930s. Chicago attracted large numbers of African American migrants from the Mississippi Delta during the Great Migration, and just as they brought their Delta blues with them—which shaped Chicago's electric blues—so did they bring their open-pit barbecue traditions, which influenced a distinctive South Side style. Playing into this development was the fact that for most of the early 20th century, Chicago was the center of the country's meatpacking industry; at one point it processed more meat than any city in the world. Surplus was so plentiful that stockyards used to give away rib tips, studded with chewy cartilage, for free.

Pork was the barbecue meat of choice in the South, and so it was in Chicago, in particular the cheap parts and preparations of pig (spare ribs, rib tips, and hot links), which cooked relatively quickly. Then and now, the meat was drenched in a sweet but tangy sauce—South Side barbecue sauce is almost always tomato-based—and served with fries and a piece of white bread to soak up the excess sauce. Orders are also typically accompanied by a small paper cup filled with creamy coleslaw, placed between the meat and fries.

The traditional Southern-style brick pits used to smoke the meat were frowned upon by the city's health department—they were impossible to clean properly—and in the 1950s gave way to what's called an aquarium smoker, made of steel and glass, invented by a local metal

 stacks of firewood outside Trice's Original SLAB BBQ

Lem's Bar-B-Q

barbecue ribs from Lem's

fabricator. This unusual pit style—a hallmark of South Side barbecue—indeed looks like a huge fish tank. The pit attaches to a smokestack that billows out waves of savory aromas that will lure you from blocks away, and delivers piquant flavors that balance the richness of the meat. Hickory is the wood of choice, although some pitmasters will mix in oak, too.

My grandmother's house in Chatham was right near two classic spots: Barbara Ann's and Lem's, to which I owe my South Side barbecue education (along with my great aunt's expert outdoor grilling). While Barbara Ann's BBQ is now sadly closed, **Lem's Bar-B-Q** (311 E. 75th St., 773/994-2428, http://lemsque.com), opened in 1954 and is thankfully still around to show everyone how it's done. Many consider Lem's the best barbecue in the city, with its quality cuts and zingy, vinegar-based sauce. This family-owned institution, which proudly displays the city's largest aquarium smoker in its windows, typically has lines that snake down the street. Going early in the afternoon on a weekday is your best bet for avoiding them. The classic rib tip and hot link combo is the essential Lem's order.

Bronzeville's **Honey 1 BBQ** (746 E. 43rd St., 773/285-9455) has earned a loyal follow-

▲ Trice's Original SLAB BBQ

ing and has a homey vibe. Neon pig signs mark the exterior, and inside the walls are covered with photos of local fans like singer and actor Jennifer Hudson. The father-son team behind the eatery serves up juicy hickory-smoked rib tips, ribs, hot links, and—unusual for the South Side—pulled pork. The ribs are the most popular item but I like the juiciness of the barbecue chicken. They also offer fried fish, chicken, and burgers that are quite good.

Trice's Original SLAB BBQ (1918 E. 71st St., 773/966-5018, www.slabbbq.com) operates out of a small storefront in the South Shore that displays stacks of wood, in case you couldn't tell that it offers authentic hickory-smoked barbecue. The family-run restaurant draws fans with its St. Louis-style ribs (meatier cuts from the hog's belly) and an impressive lineup of sides (greens, mac 'n' cheese, and spaghetti) to go along with the trinity of ribs, rib tips, and hot links. Slab's also serves smoked turkey legs, which are marinated for 14 hours; they sell out fast, so call ahead if you want one.

5 Stroll the street art in Pilsen

Neighborhoods and City Streets • Arts and Culture • Museums

Why Go: Get in touch with Chicago's Mexican community through its murals.

Where: Neighborhood roughly bordered by W. 16th St. in the north and I-55 in the south, extending east from S. Ashland Ave. to the Dan Ryan Expy. • L train Pink Line to 18th St.

Timing: Spend a half day seeking out murals and exploring the museum, and give yourself time to grab a bite. Visit around Día de los Muertos (Nov. 1-2) for an especially atmospheric visit.

As soon as you step onto 18th Street, the dynamic energy of Pilsen greets your senses. The scent of *conchas* (shell-shaped sweet bread) and *elote* (grilled corn) wafts from bakeries and street carts. In summer, you'll hear the tinkle of bells announcing *paleteros* selling ice-cream pops or, when it's colder, blasts of the steam whistle from a *camote* (sweet potato) cart blowing through the streets. Bold murals brightening buildings and alleys catch your gaze everywhere you go. Pilsen has more public art than any other neighborhood in Chicago. When the Mexican community first started moving here in the 1950s, displaced from elsewhere in the city, they were surrounded by Baroque architectural reminders of Pilsen's then-predominant residents, who gave the neighborhood its name and hailed mostly from the Czech Republic. The new arrivals marked their new home with vibrant murals.

Walking along **18th Street** is an easy route for mural-seekers, and **16th Street** also boasts plenty of street art. I always start at the L's **Pink Line 18th Street Station stop** (1710 W. 18th St.), where a mosaic featuring Aztec symbols lines the walls and stairs; artist Francisco Mendoza and students from Gallery 37 created it to celebrate Pilsen's Mexican heritage.

Walk a few blocks east to find Taqueria Los Comales (1544 W. 18th St.); the eatery's eastern side features **Reach for Peace,** an elaborate mural by Yollocalli Arts Reach, an initiative of the National Museum of Mexican Art. It illustrates kids, buildings (both traditional houses and modern developments), and oversized hands grasping in a handshake, in a call for solidar-

DECLARATION
of IMMIGRATION

WE ARE A NATION OF
IMMIGRANTS

NO INHUMANE TREATMENT
DEPORTATION
FAMILY SEPARATION
DETENTION

NO WALL

NO HUMAN BEING
IS ILLEGAL

NATIONAL SECURITY
IS USED TO FOSTER

Declaration of Immigration mural is a collaboration between Salvador Jiménez-Flores and students with Yollocalli, a youth program of the National Museum of Mexican American Art.

37

Tips for Eating in Pilsen

After art, Pilsen is most noted for its culinary treats. You can't go wrong at most of the little diners and street carts, but I recommend **5 Rabanitos** (1758 W. 18th St., 312/285-2710, http://5rabanitosdotcom.wordpress.com) for a taste of contemporary Mexican cuisine. The kitchen is led by chef Alfonso Sotelo, who trained under celebrity chef Rick Bayless. Here you'll find fresh, well-presented dishes without a hefty price tag (the *pescado en mole verde* is my go-to). Or, for an authentic adventure, head to **Birreria Reyes de Ocotlan** (1322 W. 18th St., 312/733-2613), which specializes in the spicy goat stews that are the hallmark cuisine of the Mexican state of Jalisco. The popular hole-in-the-wall also serves goat *cabeza* (head) and *lengua* (tongue) tacos. Sprinkle the goat meat with lime to cut the richness.

ity within a community that has battled against gang violence and gentrification. The mural faces new cafés and high-priced restaurants that have crept into the neighborhood.

Another block east, the Frida Room (1454 W. 18th St.) showcases a feminist take on *Lotería,* cultural depictions of which are scattered all over Pilsen. In the traditional Mexican card game, each card features an image and a name. Called ***La Valiente***—after the card that typically represents "the brave man"—the café's mural instead features a woman in a sombrero, serape, and bandolier holding ammunition. Inside there's more art, with colorful paintings of Frida Kahlo and *luchadores* (Mexican professional wrestlers). Across the street, Memo's Hot Dogs (1447 W. 18th St.) also has a *Lotería*-inspired mural, an image of ***La Dama*** ("the lady") with a flirty expression. On the side of the building is a lighthearted mural of **Cheech and Chong** enjoying hot dogs.

Back across the street, one of the neighborhood's most uplifting murals can be seen at Pilsen Vintage and Thrift (1430 W. 18th St.). Created in summer 2020, the **Black and Brown Unity Wall** honors the community of Black and Brown people—but the original was destroyed the next day. The neighborhood's artists regrouped and painted another mural of glowing Black and Brown faces to rededicate the message of unity.

At the end of the block on the other side of the street is an easy-to-overlook mural painted on the side of a building in an alleyway (1413 W. 18th St.). I've seen Salvador Jiménez-Flores' mural dozens of times, but I always stop and tear up. Its title, ***Declaration of Immigration,*** is emblazoned in red and black text, and the artwork asserts in bold caps: "We are a nation of immigrants. No inhumane treatment, no deportation, no family separation, no detention. No wall. No human being is illegal."

There are many more murals—the stretch of 18th Street described takes about 15 minutes to walk without stops—but for added cultural insight, go with **Pilsen Public Art Tours** (www.ppat.space, May-Oct., $20 adults, free for children under 12), which offers hourlong walking and biking tours with local art educators. Tours can be reserved for individuals and small groups.

Top off your Pilsen exploration with a visit to the nearby **National Museum of Mexican Art** (1852 W. 19th St., 312/738-1503, http://nationalmuseumofmexicanart.org, free). This influential museum is accessible and warm, with a single floor and guides who offer translation help and answers to your questions. The permanent collection documents thousands of years of Mexican history and culture and includes 10,000 pieces ranging from pre-Colombian ceramics and artifacts to contemporary mixed media works. The special exhibits are especially fascinating and have explored everything from Mexican identities to the Baroque Mexican nun and poet Sor Juana. A visit to the gift shop, Tienda Tzintzuntzán, is a must. Its artful displays recall outdoor Mexican markets, and you can scoop up treasures like hand-woven baskets, clay sculptures, and whimsical painted figurines.

The museum also hosts an annual display of *ofrendas,* altars dedicated to departed loved ones, for **Día de los Muertos (Day of the Dead).** This is my favorite time to visit Pilsen. *Ofrendas* also start popping up on some lawns around the neighborhood leading up to the November 1-2 celebration, and browsing the variety of offerings to the deceased, from photos to food, is always interesting.

Connect with . . .

❼ Drink in local flavor at neighborhood cafés (Cafe Jumping Bean)

Groove to the Chicago blues

Chi-Town Essential • Black Chicago • Arts and Culture

Why Go: Visit the former recording studio responsible for producing groundbreaking blues albums, then catch a show at a living legend's nearby club.

Where: South Loop • L train Green Line to Cermak-McCormick Pl. (Willie Dixon's Blues Heaven Foundation) or Roosevelt (Buddy Guy's Legends)

Timing: Plan on an hour for a tour at Willie Dixon's Blues Heaven Foundation. Sets at Buddy Guy's Legends last about an hour, but factor in the possibility of staying for multiple sets. You'll need to arrive a few hours early if you want to snag a table for a show on weekends nights.

The soundtrack of Chicago is undeniably the blues. The power and simplicity of its rhythms and the grit of its moans echo the joys and hardships of life in this city. If you've never swayed to a 12-bar blues song belted out by a dynamic musician in a dim bar with liquor fumes and tightly packed fans, then you haven't experienced an essential part of Chi-Town.

Chicago blues came about as a direct result of the Great Migration. African Americans fleeing the inequality and brutality of Jim Crow rode the Illinois Central Railroad from Mississippi through New Orleans and St. Louis to Chicago, and transported their Mississippi Delta blues traditions with them. The Mississippi musicians adapted the music to the new environment during the 1930s and 1940s, electrifying their acoustic guitars so they could be heard over crowds and evolving lyrics to reflect the urban surroundings.

"Race record" labels were also headquartered in Chicago, and these companies helped shape the blues. Race records marketed Black musical forms—blues, jazz, gospel—only to African Americans from 1920 through the 1940s, until white Americans began discovering the music, and it was rebranded as rhythm and blues or rock 'n' roll. One of the legendary record labels that helped define Chicago blues in the postwar era of the '50s and '60s was Chess Records. Most of the seminal tunes associated with Chicago blues—like "Hoochie Coochie Man" by Muddy Waters, "My Babe" by Little Walter, and "Spoonful" by Howlin' Wolf—were recorded

garden terrace at Willie Dixon's Blues Heaven Foundation

Buddy Guy performing at Legends

The Great Migration: Sweet Home Chicago

The Great Migration refers to the mass exodus of African Americans from the South to cities in the North, Midwest, and West between 1916 and 1970. It was the largest mass migration in U.S. history, prompted by the violence and persecution wrought by Southern Jim Crow laws designed to uphold white supremacy. About 500,000 African Americans moved to Chicago, mainly because the Illinois Central Railroad provided a direct route from the Delta to Chicago, and plentiful factory jobs were available. New arrivals were limited to living on the West and South Sides of the city, where crowded conditions and forced segregation spurred African Americans to build their own cultural and economic landscapes, including banks, newspapers, museums, and nightclubs.

at the label's South Side studio. Songwriter, bassist, and producer Willie Dixon wrote and produced many of those tunes, and was basically the architect of the Chicago blues sound. As the years went on and the blues melody was sped up and re-named "rock," many white musicians capitalized on the music without acknowledgment or payment to the Black musicians who created it. In the 1980s, Willie sued Led Zeppelin and Atlantic Records over their tune "Whole Lotta Love" for plagiarizing "You Need Love," a song Willie wrote for Muddy Waters in 1962. Willie eventually won the lawsuit after a long legal battle.

After he died in 1992, his widow, Marie, bought the Chess Records studio with money from the suit and turned it into a nonprofit organization and tribute to the musicians who laid the foundation for American popular music. Today, you can tour the recording studio where icons sang about good times and heartaches, as well as see records, guitars, and photos from the era and hear stories about everything from Muddy's first recording of "Hoochie Coochie Man" to the Rolling Stones ode to Chess, "2120 S. Michigan Avenue," at **Willie Dixon's Blues Heaven Foundation** (2120 S. Michigan Ave., 312/808-1286, www.bluesheaven.com, tours Fri.-Sun. noon-3pm, suggested donation $15 adults, $10 ages 5-17). Hourlong tours take place on weekends, but call ahead to confirm. In summer, the former studio also hosts concerts on the outdoor terrace.

After learning about the history of Chicago blues, you'll be better able to appreciate a live show. Just under a mile and a half north, about a 20-minute walk, is **Buddy Guy's Legends** (700 S. Wabash Ave., 312/427-1190, http://buddyguy.com), a club that every Chicagoan (or wannabe Chicagoan) should visit. Buddy Guy started his career as the house guitarist for Chess Records. Today, he is the elder statesman of the blues and the most influential guitarist alive. It was from Buddy that Jimi Hendrix learned his hypnotic riffs, and it was Buddy's bombastic style that inspired the likes of Eric Clapton, Jimmy Page, Jeff Beck, and Keith Richards. Legends is his place, and that rarified blues club that rightfully attracts fans from across the globe. Don't let the many tourists deter you; this club features real blues—you will be emotionally moved and compelled to dance. Legends has two levels and hosts local as well as national acts like Bobby Rush, Shemekia Copeland, and Christone "Kingfish" Ingram. It also has a full kitchen that turns out solid Louisiana dishes, a nod to Buddy's home state. The space is decorated with Buddy's Grammys, a Rock and Roll Hall of Fame statue, and signed guitars from other musical gods like Carlos Santana and B. B. King. Buddy also typically hangs out at the bar and plays a song if he's in town.

There are free all-ages acoustic sets during the week during lunch and dinner. Over-21 shows start around 9:30pm ($10-20 cover). It's a good idea to buy tickets for weekend shows in advance. It's mostly standing room only here, so if you want a table with a seat, show up at least three hours in advance; tables usually fill up by 7pm during the week and by 6pm on weekends.

Connect with . . .

28 Wander the urban canvas at the Wabash Arts Corridor

Drink in local flavor at neighborhood cafés

Food and Drink • Neighborhoods and City Streets

Why Go: Soak up community vibes, one sip at a time.

Where: Citywide

Timing: Each of these cafés was created for lingering; plan on spending at least 45 minutes to get a real sense of place. Mornings can get a little crowded at these spots, so late afternoons are best for a leisurely visit.

As a writer often working in solitude, I enjoy cafés for the strong sense of community and inspiration they provide. These are some of my favorites, offering portals into their welcoming neighborhoods.

Filled with books and paraphernalia that conjure a jumble of far-flung escapades, **Kopi Cafe** (5317 N. Clark St., 773/989-5674, www.kopicafechicago.com)—which self-identifies as "A Traveler's Cafe"—is the sort of spot made for wandering minds and appetites. Located on a busy section of Clark Street in Andersonville, the friendly space reflects the eclectic, bohemian energy of the neighborhood. Your first clue that this is not your typical coffeehouse: the people hanging out in the café's display windows, lounging on embroidered floor pillows and low tables. Walk inside, and head past the display cases filled with cakes and tortes to find a mismatched selection of wooden tables and chairs. Clocks tell the time in Moscow, Goa, Kyoto, and Rotorua, and a bookcase lined with travel guides and narratives will tempt you to settle in for some reading. The café's menu is extensive and vegetarian-friendly. I usually order a pot of tropical green tea and the Salty Madame Salmon, a croissant sandwich with lox, egg, tomato, and Swiss cheese. Hand-crafted scarves, totes, tapestries, and maps hang above some of the tables, forming a loose trail that visually guides you to a small but overflowing boutique area in the back of the café. I love to get up and roam the international bazaar—filled with handmade soaps, incense, clothes, and jewelry, some made by the co-owner Rhonda—just inches from my

Cafe Jumping Bean

Kopi Cafe

world clocks and travel guides at Kopi Cafe

table. Kopi also becomes an intimate club on Monday nights, when it hosts live musicians while locals sip on wine, beer, and margaritas.

Cafe Jumping Bean (1439 W. 18th St., 312/455-0019, http://cafejumpingbean.word-press.com) is a community anchor in Pilsen, a neighborhood that has battled for its soul against gentrification, and a symbol of its hard-driving work ethic and Mexican American spirit. With vivid blue and red windowpanes, walls the color of papayas—accented with Aztec mosaic art—and hand-painted tables that double as domino and chess boards, this tiny spot emits pride and warmth. It offers high-quality coffee and food at low prices and also serves as an art gallery, with walls adorned by rotating pieces from neighborhood artists. Early mornings attract crowds of students and workers, but early afternoons are the sweet spot when you can relax and listen to classic *ranchera* tunes while sipping a chocolate Mexicano or the popular ChocoEspresso. My fondest memory of the café took place one late afternoon, when regulars typically hang out at the bar; the barista asked my name and introduced me to José and Memo, two silver-haired diners who regaled me with humorous exchanges as they played a vigorous game of dominoes that stretched over hours. Munching on a pesto chicken sandwich, I felt like I was in a neighbor's home.

The scent of cinnamon, sugar, and vanilla wafts through the doors of **TeaPotBrew Bakery** (1802 S. Wabash Ave., 312/966-6001, www.teapotbrewbakery.com), perfectly conjuring the inviting vibe at this small South Loop café, an oasis of calm in a fast-paced area in the shadow of I-90 that draws parents rolling strollers, bicyclists, and stylish coffee-lovers alike. At this funky and inclusive neighborhood spot, everyone really does know your name. A family-owned business that takes pride in its homemade cakes and cookies like a master baker grandma would—in fact, many recipes come from the family matriarch—this is the place to sit and savor high-quality drinks and bites without the stiff formality. Honeycomb-patterned wallpaper serves as a sophisticated backdrop for gleaming copper containers of Rishi tea, while delicate glass canisters full of herbal blends half-circle a display of colorful macaroons, muffins, and cookies. In addition to the sweet treats, there are tasty sandwiches, quiches, and soups as well as, on Sundays, chicken and waffles so good that they have been known to stir up tears of joy. I like to lounge on the patio in the back of the café, decorated with a wall of cartoon-like images of tea, donuts, cakes, and cookies. After ordering the special of the day, which usually involves a creative treat

▲ patio at TeaPotBrew Bakery

infused with tea (think scones with rooibos and lavender), I sit and people-watch. It's particularly fun to check out the purchases of customers who've ordered birthday or wedding cakes, as they usually want to show off owner Veranda's innovations to others, like one customer who happily revealed a three-tiered, rose-colored anniversary cake topped with fresh peonies.

That's what I love about these cafés; you never know when you'll connect with someone about some random thing.

Roller-skate Chicago style

Chi-Town Essential • Black Chicago

Why Go: Learn the moves of the distinct JB skating style developed on the South Side in the 1970s, or just observe practitioners of this vanishing art form.

Where: South Side • L train Red Line to 87th and then CTA bus #87 to 87th St. & Greenwood (The Rink) • L train Red Line to 79th and then CTA bus #79 to 79th St. & Racine (Dr. Martin Luther King, Jr. Park & Family Entertainment Center)

Timing: You might spot JB skaters on any given day, but The Rink's designated night is Thursday—when you can take a lesson—and your best bet at the Dr. Martin Luther King, Jr. Park & Family Entertainment Center is on Friday and Saturday nights.

Roller skating occupied a large portion of my time while I was growing up. Riding bikes and jumping rope were well and good, but nothing compared to the thrill of being in the rink. Back then, there were roller rinks all over the South Side and south suburbs, and going to one was an event—to preteens, roller rinks were like daytime nightclubs. We'd wear matching T-shirts and sport the latest hairstyles. Everyone started out renting the ugly, worn-out beige rental skates, but aspired to eventually have their own shiny white pair topped with fluffy pom-poms. Going to a rink on the South Side was about more than simply skating; it was about style and fly moves—there was a specific culture.

In the early 1970s, a distinct Chicago style of skating developed on the South Side. Inspired by James Brown's kinetic dance steps, a man named Calvin Small and his friends created a groove-heavy style that they dubbed **JB skating.** Defined by dazzling moves that went by names like "big wheel," "crazy legs," and "gangster walk," practitioners spun and moved with elastic motions, as if their limbs had no bones; they were essentially dancing with the same energy and creativity as in a club—but on wheels. I didn't know this history then, but regularly witnessed JB skating whenever I went to the rink. I learned to do the "big wheel," a lunging up-and-down motion, but always tripped over my skates when attempting the elaborate, fluid

▲ roller skaters at The Rink

▲ a couple at The Rink

footwork of the "gangster walk." But just watching JB skaters and listening to the funky tunes always provided just as much fun.

Now, there are only two skating rinks left on the South Side. **The Rink** (1122 E. 87th St., 773/221-2600, www.therinkchicago.com, $10 admission, $1 skate rentals) is the more storied. Since 1975, this Chatham institution has been the headquarters for the best JB skaters and the best DJs. Music is an important component of this skating form; if it's not the Godfather of Soul's flawless funk playing, then soul classics with heavy beats are required. Songs of choice tend to hail from the 1970s and 1980s, although hip-hop and R&B selections from the 1990s and 2000s are also popular. You might catch JB skaters on any given day—gliding across The Rink's hardwood maple floors, past walls with orange, blue, and purple stripes—but the designated night is Thursday (8pm-midnight). You can come and just watch the moves—which now also include new-school additions like flips—or arrive early for adult lessons (6:30pm-8pm, $12) and join in.

Dr. Martin Luther King, Jr. Park & Family Entertainment Center (1219 W. 76th St., 312/747-2602, www.unitedskates.com/public/chicago, $10 admission, $4 skate rentals) in Auburn Gresham is definitely more of a kids' spot, hosting school groups and birthday parties, and has bowling lanes and games in addition to its rink. For JB skating, which draws the adults rather than kids, your best bet is Hip Hop and R&B nights on Fridays and Saturdays (7:30pm-9:30pm). Tickets have to be purchased online in advance.

9 Celebrate music and history at Black Ensemble Theater

Black Chicago • Arts and Culture • Family Fun

Why Go: Enjoy dynamic musical productions by and about Black performers at a landmark Chicago theater.

Where: 4450 N. Clark St. • 773/769-4451 • http://blackensembletheater.org • $55-65 • L train Red Line to Wilson • CTA bus #22 to Clark & Sunnyside

Timing: Black Ensemble Theater produces 5-6 productions a year, and most run about two hours. Shows (7:30pm Thurs., 8pm Fri., 3pm and 8pm Sat., 3pm Sun.) can sell out on Saturdays and Sundays.

The first time I entered Black Ensemble Theater about 25 years ago, I stepped down into the cramped basement—packed with around 100 people—at the Hull House Community Center, expecting an amusing play by a small community theater. Instead, I sat electrified in my seat. As a lifelong theatergoer, I had never seen a local production capture the essence of Black culture with such authenticity and humor. There was music, there was dance, and there was history expertly melded into an engaging production. The high-energy connection between the audience and actors made it feel like a neighborhood party, where you laugh and cheer on the best dancers. The play was *The Other Cinderella,* which tells the familiar fairy tale through a Black cultural lens: The stepmomma works at the post office; the fairy godmomma is from Jamaica and demands an 11:45 (rather than midnight) curfew because "you know how we are"; the castle page is from the projects; and various other roles address economic disparity, colorism, and gender roles in between a soulful soundtrack of original songs.

It's impossible to discuss the significance of Black Ensemble Theater without exploring the background of its founder, Jackie Taylor. A legendary Chicago figure, Jackie has appeared in movies like *The Father Clements Story* (1987), *Losing Isaiah* (1995), and *Barbershop 2: Back in Business* (2004), but is most famous for her role in the classic Chicago film, *Cooley High* (1975). The film takes place in the Cabrini-Green housing projects, where Taylor herself grew up. The film's redeeming portrayal of Black high-schoolers navigating the challenges of Black Chicago

Black Ensemble Theater

in the '60s inspired her to found Black Ensemble Theater in 1976. Concerned about pervasive stereotypes in the media and racism within the theater and film industry, Jackie focuses on telling stories that illustrate the creativity and resilience of the Black community, while also supplying consistent jobs within the industry. Black Ensemble began producing original plays combining music and history in that small basement theater in the diverse Uptown neighborhood, and soon the productions were selling out. So, she raised money to build and operate the Black Ensemble Theater and Cultural Center, which opened in 2011 a few blocks west of the original location. What began as a small community organization has grown into a multimillion-dollar enterprise. The company's focus on uplifting musicals that reflect the Black experience also helps supports its mission to eradicate racism.

Taylor writes and directs many of the productions, and the company hosts a Black Playwrights Initiative to help new writers develop their works, many of which eventually land on the Black Ensemble stage. Most of the productions are kid-friendly, and the music and dance help underscore elements that might otherwise be a little hard for younger audiences to grasp.

▲ Black Ensemble Theater

The company's shows frequently document the lives of Black musical legends. Noted productions have included *Don't Make Me Over (In Tribute to Dionne Warwick), Muddy Waters: The Hoochie-Coochie Man, Don't Shed a Tear (The Story of Billie Holiday), A New Attitude: In Tribute to Patti LaBelle, The Otis Redding Story,* and *The Jackie Wilson Story,* which was so successful that it spurred Jackie to develop a national touring component for the theater. *The Jackie Wilson Story* went on to sell out four weeks at the Apollo Theater in New York, and the show gave Black Ensemble a national presence and opened up a wider audience for the Chicago theater.

Years later, in the Black Ensemble's now-sleek, 170-seat theater, I viewed *The Other Cinderella* again; the musical is such a favorite that it's produced every two years. I sank into the roomy seat and prepared to watch familiar scenes. But that wasn't the case; the prince now had a Twitter account that he used to locate Cinderella, the fairy godmother danced to Beyoncé, and Cinderella was a pro at taking selfies. The story was similar, but with updated details for a fresh take. I wasn't surprised—The Black Ensemble Theater has remained vital for over 45 years by paying attention to change while also honoring history. And although the surroundings were different this time around, with plush crimson seats, an elevated stage, and more polished set design and costumes, the fun-loving vibe was the same as ever: that of a community gathering, with lots of spontaneous audience comments and laughter.

10 Kayak the Chicago River

Get Outside

Why Go: Gain a new perspective on the city by paddling its primary waterway.

Where: Kayak Chicago rental office at 1220 W. Le Moyne St. • 312/852-9258 • http://kayakchicago.com • guided tours $70-85, rentals $30-40 per hour or $90-120 per day • L train Red Line to North/Clybourn

Timing: Kayak Chicago, and other kayak companies in the city, typically operate late May-September. Guided tours last 2-3 hours, and rentals are available by the hour or day. Reserve in advance, especially for weekends.

The Chicago River famously flows backward. During the mid-1800s, the city became an industrial boomtown thanks in part to the river, which serves as a link to the Mississippi River and the Gulf of Mexico. All that industry also created so much filth that the city's drinking water supply—Lake Michigan, into which the river emptied—was becoming polluted with sewage that spurred typhoid, cholera, and dysentery outbreaks. A startling engineering feat was the solution; three canals were constructed to reverse the flow of the river, away from the lake.

Considering this history, I'll be honest: The first time I saw people paddling the Chicago River in neon-yellow kayaks, I was horrified; only unsuspecting tourists would get into that water, I thought. But the river has been significantly cleaned up in recent years. And though I'm used to kayaking in crystalline lakes against scenic natural backdrops, when the the pandemic hit, I realized that it would be a while before I'd see bodies of water outside the city. As for many, the confinement helped me see more of the beauty in my backyard.

The Chicago River is part of a system that includes the Main Stem, North Branch, and South Branch, as well as 52 miles of constructed waterways, for a total of 156 miles that run through the city. The Main Stem cuts east-west from Lake Michigan through the Loop and is lined by the Chicago Riverwalk, near the western end of which it meets the North Branch and South Branch, which wind their way through the city's neighborhoods.

Several kayak rental companies ply the Chicago River, including a couple of convenient

▲ kayaking on the Chicago River

⬥ paddling near the Wells Street Bridge

options near the Riverwalk like **Wateriders** (500 N. Kingsbury St., 312/953-9287, http://wateriders.com), near the Riverwalk's western end, and **Urban Kayaks** (435 E. Chicago Riverwalk, 312/965-0035, http://urbankayaks.com), on the eastern end. Both offer rentals as well as guided paddling trips. But I made a reservation for an architectural kayak tour with the city's best-known outfitter, **Kayak Chicago.**

After a quick lesson on paddle strokes and kayak balancing, our small group launched into the water near the company's office, west of Goose Island. Paddling south, the first building on the skyline I recognized was the Merchandise Mart, looming ahead with outsized grandeur. Puffy, emerald-green shrubs lined the river's edge, and a few egrets landed on the sides of the East Bank Club building to watch and judge my unsteady paddling. Kayaking along, I was hit with sensory overload, with the glinting reflections of the steel skyscrapers, rumbling of cars on bridges overhead, and cruise boats spraying us in their wakes. But then you relax into it, and it's exhilarating. Our guide was great at helping usher us past large tour boats and water taxis (given the river traffic, I wouldn't recommend kayaking the river on your own unless you have a relatively high skill level) and also supplied lots of architectural history—I hadn't realized that Chicago is second only to Amsterdam as the city with the most moveable bridges in the world—but I was mostly lost in the splendor of the skyline as we neared the Riverwalk. Veering east down the river, landmarks like the twin concrete towers of Marina City and the steel-and-glass sleekness of the AMA building sprouted up on the sides of the river. A seagull actually landed on my kayak, checking me out for an entire minute. And then it was time to turn around to return to the rental office.

Paddling the river was truly unlike anything I've experienced. The panoramas of sky-scrapers surrounding you, reflected in the dark mirror of the water, are unlike any views you get on land. The urban landscape, even familiar bridges and streets like Wabash and Michigan, looked different from river level—removed but intimate—giving me a surprising new perspective on this city I've lived in and loved for so long.

11

Admire the amazing architecture of Beverly

Neighborhoods and City Streets • Arts and Culture

Why Go: View the highlights of one of the country's largest National Register historic districts.

Where: Longwood Dr. and Griffin Pl. (W. 4th Pl.) in the Beverly neighborhood

Timing: This short drive of several miles doesn't take very long—about 10 minutes without stops—but plan on at least an hour so you can go slowly or get out of the car for short strolls to better take in the architecture. Although scenic in all seasons, Beverly reaches its full leafy glory in spring and summer.

Many locals have the mistaken notion that the city's architectural treasures reside only downtown and on the North Side, missing out on the stunning structures of the far South Side's Beverly community. The neighborhood sits on the Blue Island Ridge, the highest natural point in the city; yep, it's called Beverly Hills for a reason. It's home to unusually large lots and impressively expansive homes, swaths of which comprise historic districts that have been deemed Chicago Landmarks for their architectural riches. Much of the heart of the neighborhood is also listed on the National Register of Historic Places, the third-largest urban area designated as such. A drive along Beverly's tree-lined streets makes you feel like you're rolling through a vintage movie set.

Kick off your journey at the **William and Jesse Adams House** (9326 S. Pleasant Ave.), a Frank Lloyd Wright masterpiece that's part of the National Register of Historic Places' **Ridge Historic District**. Built in 1900, it features Wright's familiar overhanging roof and broad porch, as well as double-hung windows, and is an example of the Prairie School style.

Carry on, heading south for just over a mile, to meet up with fabled Longwood Drive, noted for its landscaped beauty. A 12-block stretch, designated the **Longwood Drive District,** spans 98th-110th Streets and is dotted with palatial hilltop houses in a mix of architectural styles. From Longwood and 98th, continue south; this stretch is 1.5 miles long, a 5-minute drive or 30-minute walk one-way. You'll soon come upon the **R. W. Evans House** (9914 S. Long-

▲ Beverly's famous Givins Castle

wood Dr.), also designed by Wright. Built in 1908, its geometric design bears his hallmarks and works in harmony with the structure's exterior elevation. Continuing south, you'll spot the Colonial Revival splendor of the **Horace Horton House** (10200 S. Longwood Dr.). Constructed in 1890 and designed by architect John T. Long, the seven-room mansion boasts columns and a half-acre lawn. Just down the street is Beverly's most recognizable structure, the **Givins Castle** (10244 S. Longwood Dr.). Perched atop a hill, rising three stories high, and topped with turrets, it was built between 1886 and 1887 and is the only castle in Chicago. Its first owner was real estate developer Robert Givins, who modeled it after an Irish castle he visited (hence the local nickname, the "Irish Castle"). It's been home to the Beverly Unitarian Church (www.beverlyunitarian.org) since 1942. The castle isn't open for tours, but you can attend a service to see the interior or go during **Open House Chicago** (http://openhousechicago.org, Oct., free), an architectural festival that lets you visit properties not usually open to the public.

Driving past 110th on Longwood, you'll converge with **Prospect Avenue,** another pleasant street to roll down if you'd like—but for now turn left and then left again to start looping

▲ Horace Horton House

A U.S. Architectural First: The Prairie School

The Prairie School started in Chicago in 1905, spread to the rest of the Midwest, and eventually influenced the world. Louis Sullivan, the architect known as the "Father of Skyscrapers," rejected the use of Greek and Roman elements and advocated for the development of a uniquely American architectural style. Frank Lloyd Wright apprenticed with Sullivan and followed his call to study nature to create form. The hallmarks of the Prairie School style are structures that integrate with the landscape, including open-floor plans, strong horizontal lines, cantilevered wings, and liberal use of natural materials such as stone and wood. A small group of young architects began creating Prairie School designs not just for houses but for buildings including banks, churches, courthouses, and factories in other states and countries. By World War I, tastes became more conservative, and the Prairie School style fell out of favor by 1920.

back north on Woods Street. In about a half-mile, turn right onto 104th Place, also called Griffin Place. Park your car and walk the short street—it's less than a half-mile between Woods and Prospect—known as the **Walter Burley Griffin Place District.** It has the largest concentration of Prairie School-style houses in the city and is named after the architect who designed most of them, including the **Walter Salmon House** (1736 W. 104th Pl.) and, across the street, the **Jenkinson House** (1727 W. 104th Pl.) and neighboring **Clarke House** (1731 W. 104th Pl.), all built around 1912-1913. Griffin started his career with Wright, an influence that can be seen in the geometric designs of some of the houses.

For brochures, maps, and more neighborhood info, stop by the **Beverly Area Planning Association** (1987 W. 111th St., 773/233-3100, http://bapa.org).

12 Feast on Senegalese cuisine

Food and Drink • Black Chicago

Why Go: Sample the delicacies of this multilayered West African cuisine, available at only a few restaurants in the city.

Where: Citywide

Timing: Plan to spend about an hour dining at one of these restaurants. Senegalese food is cooked to order, so be prepared for leisurely service.

Chicago's diverse restaurant scene showcases a multitude of international options. While African cuisine isn't as visible as European, Asian, and Latin American offerings, you can nonetheless eat from one end of the continent to the other in the city; my favorite dishes come from Senegal. I discovered the delights of the country's food through its music; I love the soaring rhythms of Senegalese musicians Baaba Maal, Youssou N'Dour, and Cheikh Lo. After attending live concerts and parties, other fans invited me to house gatherings where bountiful Senegalese meals were served.

Located on the Atlantic coast of West Africa, the country crafts some of the continent's best cuisine, featuring elaborate dishes that are stewed and marinated in herbs and spices, influenced by North Africa, as well as France and Portugal. Meals often feature seafood, chicken, and sometimes lamb. Grouper, swordfish, barracuda, shrimp, and crab are popular bases for main courses, and in Chicago, tilapia and snapper are common. Dishes are often accompanied by couscous. Heaping stews and hearty, sauce-covered dishes hearken to the traditions of West Africa's Wolof people, who often share big, one-pot meals.

Senegalese people are known for their hospitality, so it doesn't matter if you're in a living room or a restaurant; you'll be treated as an honored guest. The welcoming owners of Bronzeville's **Yassa African Restaurant** (3511 S. King Dr., 773/488-5599, www.yassasenegaleserestaurant.com), Madieye and Awa Gueye, are fine examples in this regard; dining in the sunny space, accented by a mural of the African continent, you'll feel like you're being en-

▲ lamb *yassa* dish from Yassa African Restaurant

▲ Yassa African Restaurant

▲ the owners of Yassa African Restaurant, Awa and Madieye Gueye

tertained in their home. Bouncy strains of Senegalese *mbalax* dance music often play in the background, and the aroma of peppers and cumin wafts from the kitchen. When I first became aware of it, Yassa was the only Senegalese restaurant in the city. I visited practically every week to dig into the national dish, *thiéboudienne,* a grilled fish dish overflowing with spices, carrots, yams, and couscous, or else the signature *yassa* chicken, marinated in lemons, onions, and garlic. I like to wash it all down with the bright-red *bissap,* a tangy and refreshing beverage made from hibiscus flowers.

Gorée Cuisine (1126 E. 47th St.,773/855-8120, www.goreecuisine.com) is also helping further awareness of Senegalese food in the city. In an intimate space on a leafy Kenwood street—a hidden gem in an area full of fast-food joints—the restaurant serves up generous portions and tasty variations on classics, like a *yassa* dish featuring salmon rather than the traditional chicken, and a vegetarian *mafé,* a rich peanut butter stew that usually features chicken or fish but here centers around carrots and sweet potatoes. The setting is cozy, with a handful of tables, golden walls, and lively videos of young African pop stars like Daara J and Omzo Dollar often playing on the wall-mounted TV.

Badou Senegalese Cuisine (2049 W. Howard St., 773/293-6913, http://badousenegalesecuisine.com) supplies Senegalese standards, as well as interpretations of soul food and Caribbean dishes in this Rogers Park eatery with mango-colored walls and a booming soundtrack of African pop and gospel music. Dive into a traditional *thiéboudienne,* or try a *yassa* with jerk chicken or an entrée of smoked turkey, collard greens, and black-eyed peas with Senegalese seasonings like *guedge,* a smoked, dried-fish flavoring. Chef Badawa "Badou" Diakhate is always experimenting. He'll ask about your spice preference and recommend dishes, or even create one according to your taste. Don't pass up a cup of *quinqueliba* tea, an earthy West African bush tea with more antioxidants than green tea, to end your meal.

13 Listen to classic Chicago jazz

Chi-Town Essential • Arts and Culture

Why Go: Bop the night away at the city's old-school jazz clubs.

Where: Citywide

Timing: Most jazz sets last 1.5 hours.

Jazz is rooted in the blues and, like the blues, traveled to Chicago by way of the Great Migration, which began around 1916. Specifically, New Orleans-based African American musicians, who had spent years refining what was then referred to as the "New Orleans Sound," fled the city in response to increasing racism and violence toward the Black community. NOLA legends like King Oliver, Jelly Roll Morton, and Louis Armstrong flocked to Chicago. By the 1920s, the South Side was bursting with "hot jazz," noted for its improvisation; it was the first time the style was heard outside of New Orleans. From these roots, the Chicago jazz sound developed, with more solos and spotlight on rhythm, as well as fixed ensembles. Around the same time, "race records"—blues and jazz recordings made by and marketed to African American audiences—started rising in popularity and solidified the sound, with Louis Armstrong and his Chicago-based bands, the Hot Five and Hot Seven, recording and releasing genre-defining records that would spread the music across the country.

Chicago's oldest jazz club is the **Green Mill** (4802 N. Broadway Ave., 773/878-5552, http://greenmilljazz.com, $10-15 cover, cash only). When it opened in 1907, it was more of a roadhouse, and the Uptown neighborhood where it's located was lined with movie studios and known as "Hollywood by the Lake"; Charlie Chaplin would drop by for a drink. But by the Prohibition era, the Green Mill had developed into a popular jazz lounge. Al Capone, who owned a speakeasy across the street, was its most famous patron. You can still pick up that vibe at the Green Mill, with its trapdoor behind the bar (used for booze smuggling back in the day), art deco-style murals, and curved velvet booths. The 21-and-over club draws an eclectic crowd, including a mix of neighborhood regulars, tourists, and curious hipsters, with its late-night

a saxophonist at Andy's Jazz Club

Andy's Jazz Club

the iconic Green Mill neon sign

▲ a trumpet player at Andy's Jazz Club

jazz, jam, and slam poetry sessions (fun fact: the slam poetry movement started at the club). The line-up is mostly local artists, with notable past musicians including Kurt Elling, Dee Alexander, and Patricia Barber. Bands typically play from 8pm to midnight, and reservations aren't taken, so arrive before 6pm if you want a seat.

Andy's Jazz Club (11 E. Hubbard St., 312/642-6805, http://andysjazzclub.com, $15 cover) is famous for its lunch-time jazz shows in the heart of River North, a nearby treat for downtown workers in the middle of the day. It also has sets at night. Andy's has a throwback vibe, with its white tablecloths and a "Wall of Fame" featuring black-and-white photos of the club's famous performers, like Corey Wilkes and Frank Catalano. It's the only classic jazz club with a great dinner menu, offering dishes like Cajun shrimp risotto and braised beef short ribs. Open since 1951, the intimate space hosts rising local acts like Junius Paul and Isaiah Collier. You can just show up for a show if you're over 21, but dinner reservations are required for all guests under 21.

The **Jazz Showcase** (806 S. Plymouth Ct., 312/360-0234, www.jazzshowcase.com, $20 general admission) is another iconic club, which originally opened in 1947 in the Gold Coast neighborhood. Today, it's located in the South Loop's historic Dearborn Station, which dates back to the 1800s. A huge photo of Charlie Parker approvingly overlooks the small stage, and the butter-yellow walls are covered with concert posters, album covers, and publicity photos of jazz greats. Icons who have played here include Dizzy Gillespie, Sun Ra, and Count Basie. With two shows every day of the week, including a Sunday matinee—free for kids under 12 (other shows are 21-and-over only)—this is the place for serious jazz fans or those interested in learning more about the genre; reverence fills the club's expansive, dimly lit room. Performers tend to be nationally recognized musicians like Freddy Cole and Roy Hargrove and draw a more mature clientele—except during matinees, when there are lots of families with music-oriented kids. Shows sell out, so buy tickets in advance online. It's cash only at the door, but the bar takes cards. The club is BYOF (Bring Your Own Food), so pick up some takeout on your way to the show.

14 Get out to Grant Park

Chi-Town Essential • Get Outside • Family Fun

Why Go: Enjoy the abundance of offerings at this celebrated green space that defines the best of Chicago parks.

Where: Park roughly bordered by E. Randolph St. in the north and E. Waldron Dr. in the south, extending east from S. Michigan Ave. to Lake Michigan • 312/742-3918 • www.chicagoparkdistrict.com • free • L train Brown, Orange, Purple, Green, or Pink Lines to Washington/Wabash or Adams/Wabash, or Red Line to Monroe

Timing: While it's a treat to visit the park year-round, summer is its prime season, while winter brings classic ice-skating experiences.

Nicknamed "Chicago's Front Yard," Grant Park encompasses more than 300 acres and is home to classic attractions like the Art Institute of Chicago and the Museum Campus, which hosts the Shedd Aquarium, Soldier Field—home of the Chicago Bears—Adler Planetarium, and Field Museum, all of which draw the tourist crowds. While you could spend days exploring the park's indoor options, its outdoor offerings aren't to be missed. In summer, there's no better place to be than outside at Grant Park. Summer is every Chicagoans favorite season; we finally get a chance to bask in the sun after six straight months of cold (if you think the seasons of spring and fall actually exist, then you're not from Chicago), and we revel in the warmth by squeezing in as much time outdoors as possible.

One of the park's—and the city's—biggest attractions is **Millennium Park,** situated in Grant Park's northwestern corner. The park was created to commemorate the dawning of the year 2000 and opened in 2004, and its glorious public art amid the green has come to symbolize Chicago in all her scenic beauty. Those seeking selfies head to the reflective *Cloud Gate* sculpture, known as "The Bean" for its shape, and *Crown Fountain,* featuring two towers displaying LED videos in the midst of a wading pool. But I never miss out on a chance to check out the pair of open-air **Boeing Galleries,** located on the park's north and south terraces. The galleries present temporary exhibitions, typically an assortment of modern art, including fasci-

1: the climbing wall in Maggie Daley Park
2: *Crown Fountain* **3:** *Cloud Gate* **4:** Lurie Garden

nating sculptures and mixed media pieces that are exhilarating to see against the backdrop of leafy trees in summertime. When I want to escape Millennium Park's crowds, my go-to is **Lurie Garden** (220 E. Monroe St.), home to a lush assortment of greenery and colorful perennials, to stroll the footbridge and watch butterflies flit between the blooms.

Also within Grant Park, adjacent to Millennium Park, is **Maggie Daley Park,** which has a 40-foot-tall **rock climbing wall** (Memorial Day weekend-Labor Day weekend). Lessons, belayers, and gear rentals are available. You'll see both kids and adults tackling the climb, which rewards with views of the skyline and Lake Shore Drive at the top. Maggie Daley Park also boasts the city's best **playground,** with a Seussical assortment of twirling slides, footbridges, and fanciful swings—for which half-hour waits can form on weekends—and play areas for various ages, including a ship for grade-school kids.

Grant Park is also a mecca for **live events** in the summer, including signature fests like the Taste of Chicago, Grant Park Music Festival, and Chicago Blues Festival. While the Frank Gehry-designed Jay Pritzker Pavilion in Millennium Park and the Petrillo Music Shell draw lots of people with these big-name summer festivals, I enjoy the significantly less crowded **Spirit of Music Garden** (601 S. Michigan Ave.), a quaint little park with a small stage that hosts live music and dance performances. The annual SummerDance festival showcases local groups playing salsa, Afrobeat, bhangra, and house music. Dance instructors give lessons before the music starts.

A short stroll northeast of the Spirit of Music Garden is **Buckingham Fountain** (301 S. Columbus Dr.), one of the biggest fountains in the world. Although it's touristy, locals love it, too, and it often serves as a backdrop for wedding and quinceañera photos. From May-October, the fountain features recurring 20-minute light and music displays, starting at dusk.

On the park's southwestern end is **Grant Skate Park** (1135 S. Michigan Ave.), an impressive three acres featuring rails, ramps, and steps to roll down. Its smooth pavement draws skateboarders, rollerbladers, and scooter riders. Even if you don't skate, this a fun place to relax and watch the action against a lovely skyline backdrop.

While summer may be Grant Park's most magical season, winter brings its own wonders in the form of ice-skating opportunities. Millennium Park's **McCormick Tribune Ice Rink** (Nov.-Mar. weather permitting, free admission) provides a good old-school experience and

▲ Buckingham Fountain

views of the park and The Bean. Maggie Daley Park's **Ice Skating Ribbon** (Nov.-Mar. weather permitting, $5 admission) offers a more dramatic experience, looping around the park's rock climbing wall and offering views of the skyline. Both spots are iconic, with their picturesque backdrops and snow-dusted trees, so crowds are a given. The trick is to go midweek, bring your own skates, and avoid the evenings, which are the most popular times.

Connect with . . .

2 Bike the Lakefront Trail
25 See world-class Impressionist art at the Art Institute of Chicago
28 Wander the urban canvas at the Wabash Arts Corridor

15 Enjoy the cultural feast of Chinatown

Neighborhoods and City Streets • Food and Drink • Arts and Culture • Museums

Why Go: Spend time in the special world created by the city's Chinese community.

Where: Neighborhood roughly bordered by W. 18th St. in the north and I-55 in the south, extending east from the Chicago River/Dan Ryan Expy. to S. Clark and S. Federal Sts. • L train Red Line to Cermak-Chinatown • Chicago Water Taxi to Chinatown

Timing: Chinatown is compact, but budget a half-day for wandering and eating.

Whenever my friends and I wanted to have an adventure while growing up on the far South Side, we would either walk to the nearby prairie to search for cool stones, plants, and critters—or else hop the L to Chinatown. From our preteen perspective, the neighborhood offered worldly experiences. We would watch elders practice tai chi in the park, then meander down Wentworth—breathing in the spicy, dank scents wafting from different storefronts—and pick a gift shop to hunt down the weirdest toy we could find for a few dollars (it was usually something fuzzy and squeaky). Our escapades always ended at Three Happiness on Cermak; we didn't know anything about dim sum, for which the restaurant is known, but we knew we could get scads of wings and egg rolls for under $5. We'd slide into the worn seats and munch away to the staccato rhythms of Cantonese flying around us. We left with bags of fortune cookies and a sense of sophisticated accomplishment.

Just west of the Red Line L station, the **Nine Dragon Wall** (158 W. Cermak Rd.) is a highlight and convenient first stop on a ramble around the neighborhood. It's a replica of a wall in Beijing, and one of only three outside of China. According to Chinese tradition, nine is the most auspicious number, and the nine glazed-tile dragons overlay 500 smaller dragons. Nearby, at the intersection of **Wentworth Avenue** and **Cermak Road**—the neighborhood's main thoroughfares—a red and green gateway, inscribed with "Welcome to Chinatown" in both English and Chinese, greets you. Down the street, **Three Happiness** (209 W. Cermak Rd., 312/842-1964, www.three-happiness.com) remains a must-stop. I still revel in its hole-in-the-

1: dim sum **2:** Chinatown entrance gate
3: Chinatown Square shops **4:** salt-and-pepper lobster

▲ the Nine Dragon Wall

wall charm whenever I visit Chinatown. Now I order the stir-fried peapods and duck fried rice, but the fortune cookies are non-negotiable.

A newer addition sits just north. **Chinatown Square** (between S. China Pl. and S. Archer Ave., S. Princeton Ave. and S. Wentworth Ave.), a two-story outdoor mall, opened in 1993. Activists fought for this land; Chinatown had already been reduced in size by the Dan Ryan Expressway. Battling for space and equity has been a neighborhood hallmark. Chicago's Chinatown was established in the 1880s—making it the second-oldest Chinese settlement in the country—after racism and brutal treatment in California and other western states prompted the immigrants to find more welcoming cities. The city's original Chinatown was based in the South Loop, but discrimination pushed the community farther south, to its present location, around 1912. Today, the neighborhood consists of 30 visually dynamic blocks crammed with over 400 businesses and cultural institutions. My favorite spot in Chinatown Square is near the bronze dragon statue, an elegant portrayal of the fifth animal of the Chinese zodiac (and my personal sign). I like to sit on the bench behind the dragon, with its waving tail, and people-watch. All **12 zodiac animals** are scattered around the mall's plaza and serve as popular meet-up spots.

When you get hungry again, it's time for Singapore noodles at the mall's **Chi Cafe** (2160 S. Archer Ave., 312/842-9993, www.chicafeonline.com), which features eye-catching 3D decor, like vining leaves jutting out from the ceiling. Another favorite in the mall is **Aji Ichiban Snack USA** (2117 S. China Pl., 312/328-9998, http://aji-ichiban-snack-usa.edan.io). My inner preteen loves the flamboyant array of Asian candies and snacks, displayed in neat rows of clear plastic containers that make the colors pop. The best thing about this Hong Kong outpost? Free samples! But don't get too dazzled by the cuteness; the prices are steep, and shoving handfuls of candies in the plastic bags quickly adds up. Avoid the squid-flavored peanuts, if possible.

I never miss a chance to visit the **Chinese American Museum of Chicago** (238 W. 23rd St., 312/949-1000, http://ccamuseum.org, suggested donation $3-5), south of the square. It's a small community museum that packs a lot of information into a tight space. A marble tiger guards the door. The 1st-floor exhibit changes regularly, but the permanent *Great Wall to Great Lakes: Chinese Immigration to the Midwest* offers an intimate glimpse of personal journeys, featuring letters, photos, and ephemera like tickets to Chinese fan dances. On the 2nd floor, a 16-minute video, *My Chinatown: Stories from Within,* offers glimpses into the lives of Chinatown residents. There's also an awesome, brightly colored dragon, used for festivals like Chinese New Year, on display.

If it's a warm day, a pleasant way to conclude your adventures is lounging under the pagoda-style pavilion in **Ping Tom Memorial Park** (1700 S. Wentworth Ave., 312/225-3121, www.chicagoparkdistrict.com), nestled north of Chinatown Square along the Chicago River, where you can watch the kayakers and water taxis float by.

Connect with . . .

⑲ Hop a water taxi from the Loop

16 Browse community bookstores

Arts and Culture • Neighborhoods and City Streets

Why Go: These inclusive, independent neighborhood anchors foster literary as well as community engagement.

Where: Citywide

Timing: Give yourself at least 45 minutes to enjoy steeping in any one of these stores. Check websites for schedules of community events.

Chicago is a city of writers and poets, from Gwendolyn Brooks, Carl Sandburg, and Richard Wright, to Sandra Cisneros, Eve L. Ewing, and Scott Turow. Its multilayered landscape and mix of people just beg to be documented. This is a literary town, and even in the digital age, bookstores remain a vital part of Chicago communities. Much like a good bar or café, the city's independent bookstores reflect their neighborhood's sensibilities, and many also function as gathering spaces, activist sites, and creative labs.

The feminist focus at Andersonville's **Women & Children First** (5233 N. Clark St., 773/769-9299, www.womenandchildrenfirst.com) is clear from the moment you step into the shop. Female faces and figures peer out from most book covers on the maple shelves. In one corner, children's books and crafts beckon in an explosion of color. Women & Children First opened in 1979 and is one of the few feminist bookstores operating in North America. It carries about 20,000 titles, which are curated from an intersectional, trans-inclusive feminist perspective, and the shop holds writing workshops, political fundraisers, and local author events, as well as national author book signings that have included the likes of Gloria Steinem, Alice Walker, and Nicole Hollander. My favorite of the store's events is Drag Queen Story Hour, typically held during Pride month in June, when effervescent drag queens read LGBTQIA+ picture books aimed at kids 2-5 years old (though adults like me also attend). Also not to miss is the shop's poetry machine, which spouts poems for 50 cents from a gum dispenser.

Open Books West Loop (651W. Lake St., 312/475-1355, www.open-books.org) is a

Women & Children First

sprawling used bookstore—which also stocks some new books—that carries approximately 50,000 titles covering endless genres, with large children's and young adult sections. Big, upholstered chairs and reading nooks are scattered around the store, making it easy to spend hours here when you only planned on a quick drop-by. Open Books is also the only Chicago bookstore that participates in Dolly Parton's Imagination Library program, which mails books every month to children ages 0-5 who live in book deserts. That's enough to earn my lifelong devotion, but that's not all that this nonprofit shop does for Chicago literacy. Other programs include Reading Buddies, which pairs second- and third-graders with volunteer reading coaches twice weekly; Creative Writing Club, which encourages aspiring authors in grades 4-12; and Wordshop, a guided workshop for young writers, after which they can pick out a free book from the store and receive a printed anthology of their class's work. As a volunteer writing coach for Wordshop, I can't begin to express the inspiration and joy I gain from guiding kids through the writing process.

The Underground Bookstore (1727 E. 87th St., 773/768-8869, www.underground-

▲ Open Books West Loop

bookstore.com) is a South Side institution. Since 1992, owner Brother Yoel has supplied books on Black history, culture, and politics to the community. Besides being an information resource, the Chatham bookstore is also an informal school. Brother Yoel has read most of the titles on the shelves of this intimate shop and offers book recommendations that will educate you on practically any topic you throw out, not to mention engage you in impromptu discussions; on visits to pick up a specific book, I've gotten pulled into hour-long debates about African history. The store also offers lectures on African diaspora history, culture, and dietary principles. Recordings of speeches by Fred Hampton, Malcolm X, and Martin Luther King, Jr., are available, as is an impressive selection of Black children's books.

West Town's **Occult Bookstore** (2032 W. Grand Ave., 773/292-0995, http://occultbookstore.com) opened in 1918 and is the oldest metaphysical bookstore in the country, as well as a Black-owned business. It carries rare books, some dating back 100 years—antiquarian books are a specialty—along with cauldrons, crystal balls, and tarot decks. Glass jars hold herbs, rare crystals line a counter, and mason jars filled with "spells in bags" are on display. Here, you can pick up obscure books, like Aleister Crowley's original 1929 edition of *Magick in Theory and Practice,* or energy stones reputed to transport you to another dimension. The shop's owner, Louvel Delon, is a houngan—a Vodou priest—and can offer guidance on everything from esoteric Eastern practices to how to get yourself on the "right magical path."

17 Hang out in happening Hyde Park

Neighborhoods and City Streets • Arts and Culture

Why Go: Check out music, arts, and cultural events in the South Side's most eclectic creative community.

Where: Neighborhood roughly bordered by E. 51st St./Hyde Park Blvd. in the north and Midway Plaisance in the south, extending east from S. Cottage Grove Ave. to Lake Michigan • L train Red or Green Line to Garfield and then CTA bus #55 to 55th St. & Dorchester

Timing: Devote an afternoon to Hyde Park, ideally in summer when it's in full swing.

With leafy streets, imposing Gothic buildings, and bubbling energy, Hyde Park has a distinctive vibe. It's not just the weighty presence of the University of Chicago and the Museum of Science and Industry, but the neighborhood's cultural mix of artists, musicians, and African American tastemakers who give it spark. If I'm spending a day hanging out on the South Side, it's typically in this neighborhood.

Hyde Park's cultural vivacity really shines in summer. You'll see artists painting murals and musicians and rappers playing or rhyming on corners or in Harper Court plaza off **53rd Street,** one of the neighborhood's main thoroughfares. The summer season kicks off with the **57th Street Art Fair** (5631 S. Kimbark Ave., 773/234-3247, www.57thstreetartfair.org, first weekend in June, free), which showcases a variety of art, jewelry, and crafts. But the real appeal is the crowd: Artists, activists, tourists, families, and fly locals all mingle on the grounds at and around Ray Elementary School, off **57th Street,** another of Hyde Park's main drags. The season peaks with the **Silver Room Block Party** (www.silverroomblockparty.com, third Sat. in July, free), an uplifting, kid-friendly, and inclusive celebration that spotlights the independent and Black creators who are routinely left out of the city's big festivals. Live music, theater and poetry performances, art and food vendors, and good times take place all day and into the night.

The annual block party is organized by **The Silver Room** (1506 E. 53rd St, 773/947-0024, http://thesilverroom.com), a must-stop any time of year. Offering well-curated tees, accesso-

Silver Room Block Party

The Silver Room

The Mayor of Hyde Park

If you spend even a small amount of time in Hyde Park, you will likely see "the mayor," aka Mario Smith, strolling down 53rd in his signature baseball cap, holding court in The Silver Room, or managing the box office at The Promontory music venue. A poet, activist, and radio host of *News From the Service Entrance* on WLPN-LP (105.5FM), Mario has been on the pulse of Hyde Park community happenings for 20 years; hence his nickname. An astute observer of Chicago's legendarily dirty politics, he always seems to know who and what you should be paying attention to. You might catch him hosting the Silver Room Block Party in the summer or teaching kids poetry during the school year. If you come to Hyde Park and spot him, don't be afraid to say hi; the mayor always welcomes visitors.

ries, and gifts, this Chicago institution is both a store and a community center, also hosting other events during the year, like listening parties, book readings, and art exhibits. West down 53rd is **Hyde Park Records** (1377 E. 53rd St., 773/288-6588), which I've been visiting since I was a teen. This tightly packed storehouse sells classic soul, jazz, house, rock, blues, and hip-hop CDs and DVDs, but the treasures are the hard-to-find vinyl albums. Turntables in the back let you listen before you buy, so what you imagine will be a quick stop can easily turn into hours. The shop also has a great collection of old *Ebony, Word Up!, Right On!,* and *Tiger Beat* magazines. Another few doors west is **Kilimanjaro International** (1305 E. 53rd St., 773/324-4860, http://oneofakindafrica.com), a boutique bursting with cultural treasures, including African apparel, jewelry, and art; it's like an urban bazaar. Friendly owner Mama Rose always makes sure you discover something you didn't know you needed.

On the neighborhood's northern edge is the **Hyde Park Art Center** (5020 S. Cornell Ave., 773/324-5520, www.hydeparkart.org), a go-to for inventive exhibits and accessible cultural events and workshops. One notable multimedia exhibit featured here was *The Tokyo Show: Black & Brown Are Beautiful,* which explored cross-cultural solidarity through films, textiles, photography, and paintings.

For a drink and a snack at the ultimate South Side dive bar, head to **Woodlawn Tap** (1172 E. 55th St, www.josephsittler.org/jimmys) on **55th Street,** also a primary pathway in this bohemian 'hood. Often simply called "Jimmy's" after its late owner, this is the place for no-

▲ bluesmen Billy Branch and Don Kinsey at the Logan Center

frills drinks and good conversation, drawing a mix of U of C students and old G Hyde Parkers. I usually grab an amaretto sour and veggie burger and get into an existential discussion with the bartender, or else sit at one of the window-side tables and just listen to other conversations. Grizzled jazz musicians often play on the bar's small stage. I often stop here before catching a blues show at the University of Chicago's **Logan Center** (915 E. 60th St., 773/702-2787, http://logancenterblues.org). The cozy venue is a good place to catch live jazz, art exhibits, and cabaret as well.

Connect with . . .

㉑ Eat your way down 53rd Street

㉗ Catch the views from Promontory Point

㉝ Appreciate Chicago's Black roots at the DuSable Museum of African American History

18 Chow down on classic Chicago eats

Chi-Town Essential • Food and Drink

Why Go: You have to eat sometime—and these dishes are Chicago requirements.

Where: Citywide

Timing: Expect to spend an hour minimum at any of these venues.

First things first: If you are a fat-avoiding carb-watcher, Chicago cuisine is not for you. While this celebrated city offers plenty of fresh, healthy dishes, none of them qualify as classics. This is the city of big shoulders and big appetites. There are plenty of arguments about the best versions of these staples, but I won't entertain them; here are the ones that everyone should try at least once.

You are not allowed to live in Chicago if you don't eat **deep-dish pizza.** Visitors are given plenty of options in every neighborhood and airport terminal. But the hands down best classic deep-dish is at **Pizzeria Due** (619 N. Wabash Ave., 312/943-2400, www.pizzeriaunodue. com). The second location of the Pizzeria Uno empire—founded by Ike Sewell, who reportedly created the deep-dish style in 1943—delivers an authentic experience: a perfectly crisp crust the thickness of a New York bagel, with gobs of cheese that ooze out in warm strings when you bite into it. The location, in the basement of a River North mansion with walls covered in framed photos of Chicago icons, is part of the charm. Pizzeria Due is usually packed with tourists, so try to go on a weekday around 5pm before the dinner rush. If you go after 5pm or on a weekend, expect to wait 45-60 minutes. But it's still better than the endless waits at the original Pizzeria Uno, located in a cramped space a few blocks away. These two pizzerias spawned the national chain, but understand that they are different from the franchises; you have to visit one of these original pizzerias to taste real Chicago deep-dish.

There are some Chicago classics you can only get in certain neighborhoods; the **gym shoe sandwich,** or **"The Jimmy,"** is one of these. It's not for the gastronomically timid—you need big hands and a hearty attitude to tackle it. The quintessential South Side sandwich—long

1: Chicago-style hot dog **2:** Pizzeria Due
3: Stony Sub **4:** deep-dish pizza

and angular like, yep, the sole of a gym shoe—is piled with roast and corned beef as well as gyro meat (lamb), grilled together and topped with onions, cheese, tomatoes, mayonnaise, tzatziki sauce, and *giardiniera* (pickled vegetables) on a sub roll. How the gym shoe sandwich originated isn't clear, but its popularity is. They're sold at sub shops all over the South Side, but the best version is at **Stony Sub** (8440 S. Stony Island Ave., 773/978-4000). This 24-hour Chatham takeout joint is cash only, but you'll be rewarded with aluminum-wrapped joy. Weekend afternoons are busiest, but the line moves quickly. To savor the sandwich while it's warm, head just over a mile east to Jesse Owens Park (8800 S. Clyde Ave.), sit on a tree-shaded bench, and enjoy.

Another neighborhood specialty that's grown into national prominence is the **jibarito.** This delicacy features thinly sliced and seasoned steak, lettuce, tomatoes, cheese, and garlic mayo on two smashed, green, fried plantains. You'll now find it on menus in cities from New York to Miami, but the original was created by Juan "Pete" Figueroa in 1996 for Borinquen, his restaurant in the Humboldt Park neighborhood, the center of the city's Puerto Rican community. Borinquen is no longer open, but jibaritos continue to be popular in the area. Check out **Papa's Cache Sabroso** (2517 W. Division St., 773/862-8313, www.papascache.com), which serves a flavorful version accompanied by *arroz con gandules* (rice with pigeon peas). Grab a seat on the patio and watch the action on Division Street.

An all-beef dog piled with mustard, relish, onions, tomatoes, a pickle spear, sport peppers, and celery salt on a poppy-seed bun, the **Chicago-style hot dog** is a highly specific delicacy—any deviation from these ingredients and it's not a Chicago dog. Originally called the "Depression Sandwich," it was reportedly invented at the now-defunct Fluky's on Maxwell Street in 1929, serving as a cheap, quick meal for factory workers and road crews. There are lots of spots to enjoy a Chicago dog, but the ultimate is at Norwood Park's **Superdawg Drive-In** (6363 N. Milwaukee Ave., 773/763-0660, www.superdawg.com). Opened in 1948 by a newlywed couple who had just graduated from Northwestern University, the eatery features a roof topped with 12-foot-tall hot dog statues (Flaurie and Maurie), who are as much Chicago landmarks as the flavorful housemade beef dogs that are always served with crinkle-cut Superfries. Eat inside at the counter, outside at tables—or order from the intercom and a carhop will bring your dog to your vehicle.

During the early 20th century, Italian immigrants working in the stockyards would bring home the cheaper cuts of beef and slow roast and simmer them in Italian spices to make them tastier. The beef was then sliced thinly across the grain and served on rolls to help it last longer. Al Ferreri claims to have invented the **Chicago-style Italian beef sandwich** in 1938. He needed to stretch a beef roast to serve 150 at a wedding. Regardless of whether his was the first or not, his **Al's #1 Italian Beef** (1079 W. Taylor St., 312/226-4017, www.alsbeef.com) still serves the best, a standout for the quality of its beef and au jus (Al calls it "gravy"). Al's has grown into a small chain around the city, but this Little Italy stand is the second location of the original eatery, which was bought out for urban renewal. Order the sandwich "wet" if you want the gravy ladled over the bread, or choose "dipped" if you want the entire sandwich submerged (most customers do). Assume the "Italian Stance" if you want to enjoy this messy dish without covering yourself in gravy: Place your elbows on the counter, spread your legs two feet apart, lean into the counter to grab the sandwich with both hands, and bite into it over the wrapper to catch the dripping jus.

The **Original Rainbow Cone** (9223 S. Western Ave., 773/238-9833, www.rainbowcone. com, Apr.-Oct.) is an essential Chicago treat. It's an eye-popping tower of chocolate, strawberry, Palmer House (New York vanilla with cherries and walnuts), and pistachio ice creams, plus orange sherbet, that tastes like a frosty party in your mouth. Husband-and-wife Joseph and Katherine Sapp opened shop in 1926, moving to the present-day location just a few years later, and it's been passed down through three generations. Stop by the rosy-colored Beverly shop and order a cone on a slightly empty stomach if you want to finish it. Slurp up the towering cone at a picnic table in the back. The original flavors are trademarked, so you can only get one here or at the seasonal kiosk on the Navy Pier. Or wait for the annual **Taste of Chicago** (Grant Park, July, free admission) to enjoy a cone alongside other Chicago classics.

19 Hop a water taxi from the Loop

Get Outside

Why Go: Take a scenic boat ride along the Chicago River for a fraction of the cost of a formal tour.

Where: Chicago Riverwalk at the Clark Street Bridge (N. Clark St. and W. Wacker Dr.) • L train Blue, Green, Pink, Brown, or Orange Lines to Clark/Lake • CTA bus #134, #135, or #136 to Wacker & State

Timing: Rides on the Chicago Water Taxi (mid-Mar.-late Nov., weather permitting) last 10-40 minutes, depending on the destination, or you can stay on the boat to cruise the river for 40-90 minutes. Catch a water taxi in the morning or early afternoon to allow enough time to wander around your chosen endpoint and catch the boat back afterward.

There's no question that Lake Michigan, with her spectacular shoreline, is Chicago's aquatic queen. But I think of the Chicago River as the people's princess, flowing through the city's neighborhoods. There are lots of formal (in other words, expensive) ways to traverse the river, like boat tours and cruises, but I love hopping a water taxi for a similar experience with a smaller fee. **Chicago Water Taxi** (312/337-1446, www.chicagowatertaxi.com, $6 one-way, $10 all-day pass) started in 1962 as a rush-hour commuter service. In the mornings and evening rush hours you'll spot executives hopping the boat to and from their offices, but for most of the day, the boats are full of locals and savvy tourists enjoying river views.

Ogilvie/Union Station is the Chicago Water Taxi's main hub. You can grab boats en route to any of its six stops here, but the Riverwalk dock at Clark and Wacker, at the southwest corner of Clark Street Bridge, is the most centrally located for exploring. A yellow and black sign near the water's edge marks the stop. There's no ticket office at this location, so I buy in advance on the website and get a day pass to expand the possibilities of routes I might feel moved to take. (Since tickets aren't available to purchase on the boats and there isn't a ticket office at every water taxi stop, it's good practice in general to purchase online in advance.)

Step onto the bright yellow double-decker boat and head up top for open air and the best

Chicago Water Taxi against the skyline

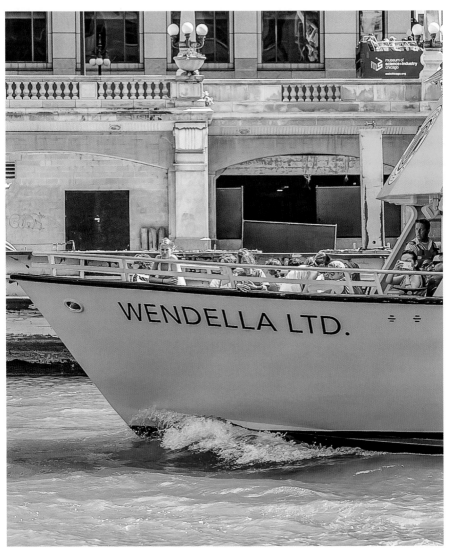

▲ cruising on the Chicago Water Taxi

views. Different boats take different routes at different times, so make sure you confirm the destination with the ticket-takers before departure. While the ride to the northernmost stop of Goose Island is entertaining, my favorite ride heads to the taxi service's southernmost stop—Chinatown—a route that takes you under the DuSable Bridge and offers great views of iconic architecture such as the stately, ivory-colored Wrigley Building. Seagulls and other birds perch on the river's edge and, in summer, purple asters, the fluffy white blooms of dogwood trees, and shiny green leaves of elm trees line the shore along the way. I love being lulled into a meditative state by the whir of the boat and watching the Chicago River's dark green waves splash against the passing white cruise boats; since these big boats narrate their tours on loudspeakers, you might even catch snippets of city history as they float past. It won't feel like 30 minutes have passed, but when I glimpse the pagoda pavilion at Ping Tom Memorial Park rising before the boat, I know I've arrived at Chinatown.

Connect with . . .

⑮ Enjoy the cultural feast of Chinatown
㉔ Ramble the Riverwalk

20 Celebrate Borinquén culture
National Museum of Puerto Rican Arts & Culture

Museums • Arts and Culture

Why Go: Visit the nation's only museum dedicated to Puerto Rican arts and culture, located in the heart of a thriving community.

Where: 3015 W. Division St. • 773/486-8345 • http://nmprac.org • free • L train Blue Line to Division and then CTA bus #70 to Division & Humboldt

Timing: Plan on an hour to visit the museum and another hour to stroll Paseo Boricua afterward.

The elegant Queen Anne turrets and gabled roofs of the National Museum of Puerto Rican Arts & Culture give it the appearance of an old-world estate. Walking down the path to its entrance, through grounds dotted with wildflowers in spring, you'll feel like you're entering another world. In many ways, you are: As part of the development of Humboldt Park, the brick and stone structure was built in 1895 as a stable and receptory for horses and wagons. The 1st floor served as the office of landscape architect Jens Jensen, who laid out the park as a pastoral paradise with rose gardens, lagoons, and green fields. Abandoned for almost 80 years, the building started undergoing restoration work in 1998, with the goal of being repurposed for the neighborhood; the museum opened to the public in 2009.

Puerto Ricans began to migrate to the city in significant numbers in the late 1940s and early 1950s, drawn by plentiful manufacturing jobs. The new arrivals mostly settled in the Lincoln Park neighborhood and established a small enclave of grocery stores and businesses. But by the 1960s, gentrification had pushed many of them out. A large portion of the population relocated to the neighborhood around Humboldt Park, concentrated on Division Street. "La Division" developed into the heart of a vibrant community, with restaurants, murals, and meeting spaces. A celebration of Puerto Rican pride and culture was organized and manifested as the neighborhood's first annual Puerto Rican Day Parade—and the next day, police shot an unarmed Puerto Rican man, Aracelis Cruz. Commonly referred to as the "Division Street riots,"

National Museum of Puerto Rican Arts & Culture

exhibit inside the museum

the uprising lasted for two days and prompted the creation of community organizations, like the Latin American Defense Organization and the Segundo Ruiz Belvis Cultural Center, to address racial inequities and provide Puerto Ricans a voice in Chicago politics. With this stronger political presence, Humboldt Park became the only recognized Puerto Rican neighborhood in the country, and a six-block stretch of **Division Street** was rechristened **Paseo Boricua,** or Puerto Rican Promenade. It's punctuated by 59-foot steel sculptures depicting the Puerto Rican flag, one at either end of the paseo. The creation of the gateway flags was spearheaded by congressman Luis Gutiérrez and then alderman Billy Ocasio, who today serves as CEO of the National Museum of Puerto Rican Arts & Culture.

You'll learn about this history and more at the **National Museum of Puerto Rican Arts & Culture.** Entering through the museum's brick archway, you're greeted in the courtyard by a colorful mosaic featuring Puerto Rican carnival iconography, such as the pointed *vejigante* masks, famously worn in the city of Ponce. The museum has four galleries that feature rotating exhibits that illuminate local and national Puerto Rican traditions. Notable past exhib-

▲ a museum display

its have included *Expresíon de Barrio,* including murals of bomba dance traditions by Puerto Rican artist Reynaldo Rodriguez and accompanied by the percussive drum sounds, and *Circo de la Ausencia,* a theatrical exhibit of circus acts and strange scenes by a San Juan theater group intended to spark discussions around political and social issues. As the only national museum dedicated to Puerto Rican arts and culture, it's difficult to experience this level of immersion outside of the island. Roam the museum on your own, or schedule a tour online—a guide will greet you on-site. The museum also collaborates with local organizations to highlight Chicago's Puerto Rican history through dance performances, poetry readings, panel discussions, and book signings. Its annual summer event, **Barrio Arts Fest,** showcases art from the diaspora. Don't miss the gift shop, which offers handmade goods from the island.

After visiting the museum, be sure to stroll down Division to absorb the sights and sounds; Paseo Boricua begins just a block east. Reggaeton and salsa usually blare from shops, and the savory smell of *sofrito,* the essential Puerto Rican seasoning mix, wafts down the street. Every other building is adorned with a mural. To learn more about the neighborhood's history and culture, you can also take an engaging walking tour with the community-based **Paseo Boricua Tour Co.** (773/676-5234, http://paseoboricuatours.com, Mar.-Dec., $25 pp).

Connect with . . .

🅗 Chow down on classic Chicago eats (Papa's Cache Sabroso)
㊱ Amble along the elevated 606 trail

21 Eat your way down 53rd Street

Food and Drink • Neighborhoods and City Streets • Black Chicago

Why Go: Enjoy Hyde Park's culinary delights, from pre-dinner drinks to dessert, on this progressive dining journey.

Where: E. 53rd St. in Hyde Park • L train Red or Green Line to Garfield and then CTA bus #55 to 55th St. & Dorchester

Timing: Budget about three hours to hit all of the spots. Start in the late afternoon or early evening; the last venue on this recommended itinerary typically closes by 9pm. Make reservations in advance for Mesler and Virtue.

There was a time when the most common option for eating in Hyde Park was of the diner/café variety. If you wanted any kind of diversity or culinary flair, you had to head downtown. Now, you can treat your palate to sophisticated cuisine at exciting eateries, most of which are Black-owned, along the concentrated eastern strip of 53rd Street.

I like to start at **Mesler** (1401 E.53rd St., 773/289-1005, http://meslerchicago.com), tucked inside the sleek Sophy Hotel. A favorite meet-up spot since the hotel opened a few years ago, the bar/lounge dazzles with decor that nods to neighborhood notables; a giant painting of former neighborhood resident and president Barack Obama adorns one wall, while metal chandeliers with geometric motifs hang over the bar, referencing the University of Chicago's scientific discoveries. Happy hour and weekends draw crowds of lively, fly locals, and an outdoor patio allures with twinkling lights, topiary trees, and fire pits. My go-to cocktail here is the 53rd Street Old Fashioned, mixed with a tasty rosemary and maple syrup. The fresh mango margarita is another good choice.

After sipping and taking in the scene, head across the street to **The Soul Shack** (1368 E.53rd St., 773/891-0126, www.thesoul53.com) for a creative appetizer. Outfitted with red tables and black upholstered chairs, the eatery serves up soul food classics like smothered chicken and short ribs, accompanied by essential sides like cornbread and greens. But you can get those dishes anywhere. The thing to order here is the innovative soul rolls: yams, greens, and

the lounge area at Mesler

salmon entrée at Virtue Restaurant

Kilwins

mac 'n' cheese—deep fried in an egg roll. The mix of flavors is scrumptious yet not so heavy that you're full after a few bites.

Then it's on to the main course. Stroll a couple of blocks east and you'll spot the brown awnings and golden letters that announce **Virtue Restaurant** (1462 E.53rd St., 773/947-8831, www.virtuerestaurant.com), owned by James Beard Award-nominated chef and 2020 Chicago-an of the Year, Erick Williams. The restaurant's menu features dishes from across the African diaspora, and the elegant, sun-filled dining room features artwork by Black artists Theaster Gates, Amanda Williams, and Raelis Vasquez. My favorite meal here is the expertly grilled salmon with white beans and turnip relish "chow chow," washed down with the French Quar-ter—a zesty blend of Pimms, meletti, orange, and lemon.

For sugar-filled decadence, follow the aroma of chocolate and fudge a block north to **Kil-wins** (5226 S. Harper St., 773/675-6731, www.kilwins.com). Although part of a chain, this es-tablishment is African American-owned. The candy and ice cream shop serves up a dizzying array of treats (the fudge samples usually have me in a sugar coma before I can even decide). I love the hand-dipped dark chocolate and sea salt caramel apple, but other standbys include a bag of the mint cookie malt balls or a New Orleans pecan praline sundae.

Connect with . . .

🔟 Hang out in happening Hyde Park

㉝ Appreciate Chicago's Black roots at the DuSable Museum
   of African American History

22 Get inspired by Black art

South Side Community Art Center

Chi-Town Essential • Black Chicago • Museums • Arts and Culture

Why Go: Visit the oldest African American art museum in the United States.

Where: 3831 S. Michigan Ave. • 773/373-1026 • www.sscartcenter.org • free • L train Green Line to Indiana

Timing: Plan to spend 1-2 hours visiting the museum or attending an event.

Overlooking the 3800 block of Michigan Avenue like a grand red-brick sentry, the South Side Community Art Center is the cultural jewel of Bronzeville. Opened in 1940 as part of the New Deal and dedicated by Eleanor Roosevelt, it's the only African American art center built during the Works Progress Administration (WPA) era to remain continuously open. Co-founder Margaret Burroughs—who would later also co-found the DuSable Museum of African American History—stood on the corner of 39th Street collecting dimes to raise money for this venue that would become the heart of Chicago's artistic Black community; eventually she and a handful of other artists and activists purchased the 19th-century mansion, and the WPA Federal Art Project supported its renovation and remodeling. In 2017, the South Side Community Art Center was named a National Treasure by the National Trust for Historic Preservation, and in 2018 it was listed on the National Register of Historic Places.

Upon its opening, the Classical Revival-style building supplied exhibition space and creative opportunities for African American artists, whose works were rarely included in galleries and museums. The center also offered art classes and community events, and was a focal point for the Chicago Black Renaissance movement of the early 20th century. Many of the era's influential artists developed and established their careers at the center. Art center co-founder and painter Eldzier Cortor was one of the first artists to exhibit here, as well as one of the first artists to make African American women the focus of his work. Gwendolyn Brooks took a modern poetry class at the South Side Community Art Center, and would go on to win the

▲ artist Makeba Kedem-Dubose at her exhibit opening

▲ gallery opening at the center

▲ the author and friends in costume for an event at the South Side Community Art Center

The Chicago Black Renaissance

While the Harlem Renaissance may be more well-known, the Chicago Black Renaissance was just as influential, leaving a profound mark on American culture. The Great Migration brought thousands of artists, writers, dancers, and musicians to Chicago, fomenting a creative movement that spanned the early 20th century. King Oliver and Louis Armstrong helped define Chicago jazz during the 1920s and 1930s, and the Delta blues was transformed into the electric Chicago blues during the 1930s and 1940s. Thomas Dorsey, a former bluesman, created the gospel music sound at Bronzeville's Pilgrim Baptist Church. In the 1930s, choreographer and dancer Katherine Dunham founded an early incarnation of her dance company, influential in its celebration of Black traditions of dance from throughout the diaspora, in Chicago. In 1936 Richard Wright founded the South Side Writers Group, and in 1940 wrote his seminal novel, *Native Son,* which he set in Bronzeville.

Pulitzer Prize—the first African American to do so—in 1950 for her book, *Annie Allen,* and become the poet laureate of Illinois in 1968. Photographer and filmmaker Gordon Parks had his darkroom in the center's basement. Elizabeth Catlett displayed some of her pivotal lithographs and sculptures reflecting the dignity of Black life in the museum's galleries. And painters Archibald Motley, Jacob Lawrence, and Charles White were all featured at the center. Children's art classes helped foster an awareness of art history and the significance of African American cultural history, which nurtured burgeoning young artists.

Whenever I ascend the art center's steep stone stairs and enter through its twin columns, I feel I'm walking on hallowed ground; floorboards creak with years of history, and the wood-paneled main gallery is dotted with thousands of pinholes representing the decades of artwork that's hung on its walls. The South Side Community Art Center hosts rotating exhibits and an ever-changing series of art-related events across two of its floors. Exhibits are dynamic, innovative, and wide-ranging, covering textiles, photography, poetry, sculpture, music, and more. Notable recent exhibits have included the last show of Eldzier Cortor, featuring his woodcuts and paintings, and *Conjuring Black Histories in Jewelry,* a display of 20th-century jewelry crafted by Black designers from across the diaspora. The center also continues to hold community events, including art classes, lively artist talks, author readings, workshops, film discussions, and spoken word events. Whether you come for an exhibit, the opening of an acclaimed artist's show, or a small workshop for teen writers, you'll find the atmosphere low-key and welcoming, with people often introducing themselves to one another and trading opinions about the work displayed.

Connect with . . .

3 Go gallery-hopping in Bronzeville

4 Savor South Side barbecue (Honey 1 BBQ)

12 Feast on Senegalese cuisine (Yassa African Restaurant)

23 Take a trip down LSD

Chi-Town Essential • Neighborhoods and City Streets

Why Go: Drive Chicago's most iconic expressway for beautiful lake and skyline views.

Where: Along Lake Michigan from Hollywood Ave. in the north to E. 67th St. in the south • www.chicagoparkdistrict.com

Timing: Lake Shore Drive is 15 miles long and should technically take only 30 minutes to drive. But that never happens (traffic, construction, gawkers); give yourself 1-3 hours to allow for a leisurely ride and some stops.

On weekends, the earlier you head out, the better; 8am is an optimum time to avoid traffic. On weekdays avoid rush-hour traffic by planning a drive between 11am and 4pm.

Cruising down **Lake Shore Drive,** drifting past beaches, parks, and people, is a quarterly requirement. The scenery is different in each season, with bikini-clad volleyball players in summer (for a balmy ride on a summer night, you might wanna put "Lake Shore Drive" by Aliotta Haynes and Jeremiah on your playlist), gold and red foliage in fall, frozen lake panoramas in winter, and blooming flowers in spring.

The 15 miles of shoreline expressway along Lake Michigan that we now call Lake Shore Drive began as an unpaved street adjacent to the Gold Coast mansion of Chicago's first tycoon, Potter Palmer. During the 1800s, it was popular for strolls and carriage rides by the wealthy neighborhood residents. As automobiles became more popular, the road was extended and paved. In 1933, it became the city's first expressway, and it was officially designated Lake Shore Drive in 1946.

I usually ride LSD from south to north; from this direction, Lake Michigan will be directly to your right as you head toward the city's skyline. Driving into **Jackson Park** at the expressway's southern terminus, you'll soon glimpse the cerulean waves of **63rd Street Beach** and, if it's summer, the aroma of barbecue will likely waft through your window—possibly accompanied by the salty, slight fishy scent of the lake. Winding around the **Museum of Science**

Lake Shore Drive

▲ Lake Shore Drive along Grant Park

and Industry takes you out of the park and past more shoreline scenes. At 55th Street is the limestone-lined strip of green beauty that is **Promontory Point,** an artificial peninsula and a nice place to stop and hop out to take in some of the best shoreline and skyline views in the city.

Continuing on through **Burnham Park,** the **31st Street Harbor** soon catches your eye; the lines of boats bobbing here recall a resort town scene rather than that of a busy city. Stop at the **Pier 31 Restaurant** (3101 S. Lake Shore Dr., no phone, Memorial Day weekend-Labor Day), located right on the adjacent **Margaret T. Burroughs Beach and Park,** and order grilled fish or a burger from the walk-up window to enjoy a meal on its deck, which has skyline views, plus live music on Fridays during summer. In spring, kites waving over the park brighten up the sky.

Next, you'll drive through **Grant Park,** and the flying saucer-shaped **Soldier Field** stadium looms ahead, signaling that you'll arrive downtown in a few minutes. Rolling by the **Museum Campus** and **Buckingham Fountain,** you'll catch some of the best iconic skyline images, especially at night when the latter is lit up. If you spot some parking, take it, and get out to snap pics of the fountain with the diamond-shaped Crain Communications Building, Vista Tower, and Two Prudential Plaza soaring in the background.

Heading out of Grant Park and over the Outer Drive Bridge, you'll catch another famous sight: **Navy Pier** jutting out into the water, capped by the giant **Centennial Wheel,** which twinkles at night. Next up is scenic **North Avenue Beach,** featuring miles of golden sand and a boat-shaped beach house set amid leafy Lincoln Park, and always packed during the day with people jogging, biking, or sunning. Soon, the Lakeview neighborhood's towering **Kwa-Ma-Ro-las totem pole,** at Addison Street, comes into view. It's one my favorite landmarks; carved out of cedar by Tony Hunt, the chief of the Kwakwaka'wakw nation in British Columbia, it rises 40 feet high and is topped by a thunderbird.

In another few miles, the blush-colored buildings of the Edgewater Beach Apartments to your left signal the end of this classic Chicago drive.

Connect with . . .

🆔 Get out to Grant Park
㉗ Catch the views from Promontory Point
㊴ Explore the Burnham Wildlife Corridor

24 Ramble the Riverwalk

Chi-Town Essential • Get Outside • Arts and Culture • Museums

Why Go: Enjoy downtown action on the waterfront.

Where: Western trailhead at E. Lake St. and W. Wacker Dr., eastern trailhead at Lake Shore Dr./Lake Michigan • www.chicagoriverwalk.us • L train Blue, Green, Pink, Brown, or Orange Lines to Clark/Lake • CTA bus #134, #135, or #136 to Wacker & State

Timing: It takes just about 30 minutes to stroll the riverfront path, but you can easily spend a day enjoying its diversions.

For years, the only time the Chicago River received attention was when it was ceremonially dyed green for the annual St. Patrick's Day Parade. Sure, you could gaze into the murky water the rest of the year and jog the few concrete paths near the river, but the waterfront didn't offer anywhere near the scenic access of Lake Michigan. Completed in 2016, the Riverwalk transformed 1.25 miles of its shoreline into a legitimate outdoor paradise, with a paved path linking gardens, public art, and restaurants. Although sometimes called "the second lakefront," the Riverwalk—which follows the Chicago River on the south side of its Main Branch through the Loop to where it meets the lake—has a more urban vibe. This waterfront area is less about recreation and more about hanging out at cafés and bars and people-watching on sunny days.

For serious exploration, start at Lake and Wacker, the westernmost access point. The Riverwalk's western end, the more developed half, comprises six coves, which are, west to east: **The Boardwalk** (E. Lake St. to N. Franklin St.), **The Jetty** (N. Franklin St. to N. Wells St.), **The Water Plaza** (N. Wells St. to N. LaSalle St.), **The River Theater** (N. LaSalle St. to N. Clark St.), **The Cove** (N. Clark St. to N. Dearborn St.), and **The Marina** (N. Dearborn St. to N. State St.).

The Boardwalk features great views of the meeting point of the three branches of the Chicago River (Main, North, and South). In The Jetty section, you'll stroll by floating gardens full of lush native plants, like swamp milkweed and mullein, that recall the city's original wet-

Riverwalk entry gate

Riverwalk stairs

land landscape. After sunset, **Art on theMART** (7:15pm-9:15pm daily Mar.-Dec.) lights up the Merchandise Mart building, just across the river, for the world's largest permanent video-projection art installation, accompanied by audio streamed through speakers. Videos of various art forms—an innovative mix including dance, music, and literature—splash across the building facade's 2.5 acres. The installation has featured scenes from the Joffrey Ballet's *The Nutcracker;* the Art Institute of Chicago's Monet paintings; puppet theater by Blair Thomas & Co.; poetry by Gwendolyn Brooks; and Cuban, jazz, and classical music. Most locations along the Riverwalk supply good views, but the best are from The Jetty.

The Marina section is home Chicago Water Taxi stops and numerous venues, including the popular **City Winery** (11 Chicago Riverwalk, 312/229-5593)—serving wines on tap and dishes like shrimp ceviche and duck tostadas. This section of the Riverwalk tends to be packed with crowds eating at umbrella-ed café tables and lounging on concrete benches.

I prefer the Riverwalk's quieter eastern half. Since it first opened, it's served as my natural respite from the rushed energy and crowded architecture of downtown. I like to sit on the steps near the **Vietnam Veterans Memorial** (between and N. State St. and N. Wabash Ave.) after a hectic day. Another favorite, farther east, is the **McCormick Bridgehouse & Chicago River Museum** (99 Chicago Riverwalk, 312/977-0227, www.bridgehousemuseum.org, May-Sept., $6), where you can sit on the bright blue chairs fronting the museum and quietly watch cruising riverboats, or head inside the museum to see the actual mechanisms of the city's movable bridges. Near one such movable bridge, the DuSable Bridge, you'll arrive at an even quieter stretch of the Riverwalk. Pause just before passing under it; this is a good spot for admiring the Wrigley Building and Tribune Tower. Nearby, above dockside cruise ticket booths, are glittering, colorful banners adorned with layers of paint, lace, and beads, waving in the wind, part of the art installation called ***...between the below...***

A bit farther east is my favorite Riverwalk joint, **Island Party Hut** (355 E. Chicago Riverwalk, 312/600-0488, May-Sept.). It's all about the atmosphere here, with thatched huts, cornhole games in the grass, and live music, and the festive vibe is contagious. While the food isn't anything special—just burgers, hot dogs, and brats—the tiki bar serves appropriately indulgent drinks, like its Lime in D' Coconut. Hang out on one of the crayon-colored Adirondack chairs and soak it all in. If you feel like being more active, **Urban Kayaks** (435 E. Chicago Riverwalk,

The Dyeing of the Chicago River

Chicago takes St. Patrick's Day seriously, with parades and the requisite guzzling of Guinness, but the most unusual celebration is the traditional dyeing of the Chicago River a bright emerald green. The origins of the event date back to 1961, when Mayor Richard J. Daley ordered use of a special green dye to pinpoint where sewage was being dumped into the river. A worker in green-stained overalls caught the attention of the St. Patrick's Day Parade chairman, who was a member of the plumbers' union, and he figured it would be fun to color the entire river green for St. Patrick's Day. In 1962, 100 pounds of the special dye was poured into the river, turning it green for an entire week. Today, the river only stays green for 4-5 hours—environmentalists lobbied against using the original harsh chemicals, so in 1966, the city switched to an eco-friendly vegetable dye. The dyeing ceremony starts at 9am on the morning of the downtown parade, which is always held the Saturday before St. Patrick's Day. Two boats go out into the river and members of the plumbers' union sprinkle an orange powder to transform it into a vivid green. Crowds gather for hours beforehand to snag a good spot to view the process. The best places to watch are on upper and lower Wacker Drive between Michigan Avenue and Columbus Drive.

312/965-0035, http://urbankayaks.com, May-Sept.), a few minutes' walk east, offers rentals and tours. At the eastern endpoint of the Riverwalk, there's extensive seating amid clusters of trees and greenery lining the river where it meets Lake Michigan.

Connect with . . .

⑩ Kayak the Chicago River

⑲ Hop a water taxi from the Loop

㊵ Taste sweet candy history (Fannie May)

25

See world-class Impressionist art

Art Institute of Chicago

Chi-Town Essential • Museums • Arts and Culture

Why Go: Marvel at one of the finest collections of Impressionist artwork found anywhere at this renowned museum.

Where: 111 S. Michigan Ave. • 312/443-3600 • www.artic.edu • $25 adults, $19 students and seniors, free for children • L train Brown, Orange, Purple, Green, or Pink Lines to Adams/Wabash

Timing: Honestly, you could spend all day in the museum, but for a focus on just the Impressionists, allow 2-3 hours.

Founded in 1879 as a museum and school and based in its current home—a building constructed for the Chicago World's Fair—since 1893, the Art Institute of Chicago today comprises one million square feet of space and 300,000 artworks and artifacts that it displays in 30 rotating exhibits. Construction of its Modern Wing in 2009 made it the second largest art museum in the country, second only to The Met in New York. While the institute's collection spans countries and centuries, it's particularly acclaimed for its Impressionist works, a focus on which makes a fine entry point to what can be an overwhelming abundance of riches.

Viewing the feather-light delicacy and complexity of the Impressionists never fails to lift my spirits. I love that Chicago is home to one of the largest holdings of their works in the world, and I especially enjoy showing it off whenever my French friends are in town, like it's my own private collection. I usually start with the Monets; the Art Institute of Chicago holds the biggest collection of work by **Claude Monet** outside of Paris, influenced early on by Chicago-based collectors like Bertha and Potter Palmer—who also built much of downtown, and who started acquiring the artist's work when he was still new and considered radical; they donated their extensive collection to the museum. Among my favorite of his paintings are the tranquil *Water Lily Pond,* with its blend of greens, blues, and pinks that give the illusion of iridescence, and *The Beach at Sainte-Adresse,* with a bright blue boat, amid an overcast sky and sandy shoreline,

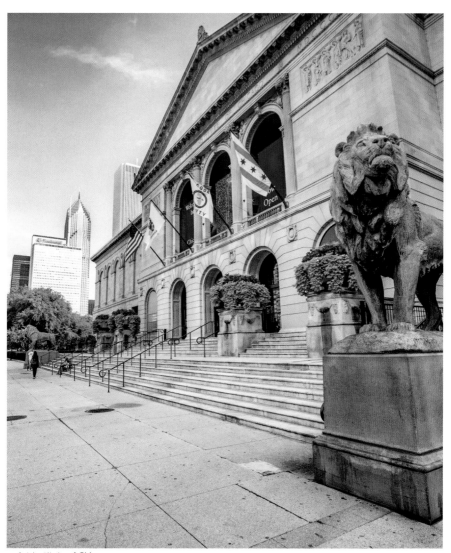
Art Institute of Chicago

1: *Acrobats at the Cirque Fernando* by Pierre-Auguste Renoir **2:** *The Millinery Shop* by Edgar Degas **3:** *Water Lily Pond* by Claude Monet **4:** *On a Balcony* by Mary Cassatt

that looks so real you want to reach out and touch the tip of it. His works are displayed in the museum's main building on the 2nd floor (Galleries 201, 205, 243, and 249).

More Impressionist artworks are spread among the 2nd-floor galleries, including some of the celebrated ballerina paintings by **Edgar Degas** (Gallery 226). I especially love *Ballet at the Paris Opéra,* rife with the ethereal beauty of dancers en pointe. But the painting that really pulls me in is *The Millinery Shop,* featuring a woman—possibly a creator, or a customer trying on hats—in a scene infused with autumnal hues; the contemplation on her face inspires me to imagine different narratives about her life.

The vibrant colors and sense of joy that define the works of **Pierre-Auguste Renoir** (Gallery 201) hold pride of place for me. *Acrobats at the Cirque Fernando (Francisca and Angelina Wartenburg)*—featuring two circus girls standing in the ring with playful stances, as one cradles a bunch of oranges tossed in tribute while more of the fruit rolls around their feet—makes me grin every time.

I like to conclude an Impressionist tour at the museum by visiting the artwork of **Mary Cassatt** (Gallery 273). Cassatt was often the only American among French artists to be featured in Impressionist exhibits. Her skill at evoking the connection between mothers and children is exceptional; ironically, she was a feminist who never married or had children, defying her family by studying art in Europe and becoming an independent artist. In *On a Balcony,* she captures a sense of female independence and confidence in her depiction of a woman in a morning dress, surrounded by flowers in a garden setting, as she reads a newspaper.

Connect with . . .

6 Groove to the Chicago blues

14 Get out to Grant Park

28 Wander the urban canvas at the Wabash Arts Corridor

26 Paddle and play in the water at Montrose Beach

Get Outside • Family Fun

Why Go: Skyline views, a protected cove, and rentals right on the beach make this a perfect spot to SUP or kayak on Lake Michigan.

Where: 4400 N. Lake Shore Dr. • 312/742-3224 • www.chicagoparkdistrict.com • L train Red Line to Lawrence or Wilson • CTA bus #78 to Montrose & Marine Dr.

Timing: Chicago beaches are open Memorial Day weekend through Labor Day. SUP and kayak rentals are available on Montrose Beach by the hour or day.

If you want to enjoy the water and outdoor activities rather than primp among the rowdy crowds, forget about the more popular North Avenue and Oak Street Beaches; Montrose Beach is the place for you. It's the largest beach in the city—stretching a little over two miles—and has a real neighborhood feel, with an unfussy, fun-loving vibe, adjacent to the Uptown neighborhood and flanked by a dog park and skate park. Community cookouts and family gatherings in the grassy area around the beach are a common sight, as are lots of parents chasing screaming kids who are splashing around and playing in the sand, teens blasting top 40 hits, sun worshippers, volleyball games, and vendors winding through the sand selling cotton candy and *paletas*.

Montrose Beach is also a great place for water sports. A seasonal rental kiosk run by **Kayak Chicago** (beach at Montrose Ave., http://kayakchicago.com) has stand-up paddleboards ($30 per hour, $90 per day) and kayaks ($30-40 per hour, $90-120 per day). Nearby is a protected cove, created by Montrose Harbor, making this an ideal spot for swimming and paddling. From here, the pretty panorama of skyscrapers to the south are set against Lake Michigan's shimmering waters and summer's blue skies.

Montrose Beach is also one of only two Chicago beaches where surfing is permitted. In winter, you might even spot a few hardcore surfers riding waves in wet suits.

When you want a break from water sports, head to **The Dock** (200. W. Montrose Harbor

▲ Montrose Beach

Dr., 773/704-8435, www.thedockatmontrosebeach.com, Memorial Day weekend-Labor Day), a beachfront café with outdoor seating and live music. Order the fish-and-chips and a beer.

Montrose Beach also has an adjoining nature preserve, **Montrose Point Bird Sanctuary.** A top birding spot in the state, this 15-acre natural habitat, featuring dunes and native plants, hosts many migratory birds—more than 300 species have been recorded here. Look out for roosting owls, sandpipers, and red-throated loons. You can spot birds year-round, but spring and fall migrations bring the most variety. Seasonal wildflowers and butterflies add to the scenery, and the skyline is stunning from this southernmost vantage.

I like to enter at the long beach's northern tip, where a taco stand sits and other vendors sell fresh-cut fruit and snow cones, but the rentals and beach restaurant are located at the southern end. Bathrooms are located at both the northern and southern ends of the beach.

Connect with . . .
② Bike the Lakefront Trail

27 **Catch the views from Promontory Point**

Get Outside

Why Go: Find one of the city's prettiest shoreline and skyline views at this parkland peninsula.

Where: 5491 S. Shore Dr. • www.chicagoparkdistrict.com • L train Red or Green Line to Garfield and then CTA bus #55 to S. Hyde Park & 55th St. • CTA bus #6 to S. Hyde Park & 55th St.

Timing: Promontory Point is the spot to catch the best sunrises in the city, although it's generally a great place to come during the day to enjoy the natural space and stellar views.

There are few South Siders who don't know about "The Point." Before the city's green spaces were expanded and updated, this was where people flocked for peaceful respites, picnics, prom photos, romantic dates, and weddings. None of that has changed; it's just that more options have made Promontory Point, which opened in 1937, something of an under-the-radar spot. Situated along the Lakefront Trail, the park is popular with walkers and bikers, but rarely as many as you'll see farther north. Stretching out into a point that dips into Lake Michigan and flanked by a turret-topped field house—built to serve as a hub for cultural and recreational programming—this piece of land on the edge of the Hyde Park neighborhood possesses striking beauty.

Promontory Point is an artificial peninsula created from 12 acres of landfill. It was designed by landscape architect Alfred Caldwell with flowering trees and shrubs, a raised meadow, a limestone seawall, and circular stone cubicles called council rings—a design element favored by Jens Jensen, with whom Caldwell worked closely, to encourage people to sit and gather—that are today used as fire pits (the only ones permitted in the Chicago Park District). At the entrance to the park, near the Lake Shore Drive pedestrian underpass, is the David Wallach Memorial Fountain, one of the point's hallmarks. An animal lover, Wallach died in 1894 and in his will left a donation to commission a fountain for "man and beast," resulting in this unusual marble fountain topped by a bronze sculpture of a curled-up fawn and featuring a ground-level pool for birds and dogs and two drinking fountains for humans.

I like to walk the park's paved pathway right up to the seawall, sit on one of the limestone blocks, and watch the waves. From here you can see the city skyline to the north in all its dreamy glory. The panorama is stunning in every season. In spring, the greenery is lush and the lake is clear from melting ice. In summer, the lake takes on an aquamarine color and shimmers against the skyline. Fall brings gorgeous gold and red foliage that contrasts with the darkening lake. Winter, surprisingly, delivers my favorite scenes; it's always freezing, so few people are in the park—affording the snow and glistening trees surrounding the frosted lake a solemn beauty.

Connect with . . .

2 Bike the Lakefront Trail

17 Hang out in happening Hyde Park

21 Eat your way down 53rd Street

▲ view from Promontory Point

28 Wander the urban canvas at the Wabash Arts Corridor

Neighborhoods and City Streets • Arts and Culture

Why Go: Discover art in unexpected places in this neighborhood mural gallery.

Where: Streets and alleys surrounding S. Wabash Ave. in the South Loop • http://wabashartscorridor.org • L train Red, Green, or Orange Lines to Roosevelt

Timing: While it would only take about 40 minutes to walk a loop around this corridor, give yourself a leisurely 2-3 hours.

The first time I stumbled onto a mural in the Wabash Arts Corridor, I was rushing to a meeting. Glimpsing splashes of color on an alley wall, I stopped to gawk. Blue and slime-green splatters poured out of a soft blue volcano with a smiling face. I had to scurry off to my meeting but made a mental note to come back and investigate. Why was this weird painting in an alley? What did it mean?

I learned that the mural, fittingly called **Slime Mountain** (623 S. Wabash Ave.), was by Columbia College alumna Heidi Unkefer and part of an initiative started by the college in 2013 to bring the arts into the everyday experience of the city's residents. A "living urban canvas," the Wabash Arts Corridor is intended to grow and evolve. Murals currently cover more than 40 buildings near the college in the South Loop, centered around **Wabash Avenue.** Local and internationally acclaimed artists have joined students and alumni to create the arresting pieces, many of which are woven into the architectural landscape in ways that surprise—you might spot one as you're walking into a parking garage or looking out a window toward a neighboring building. When I finally returned to the corridor again about a year later, a whole crop of new art greeted me. Over the years, I've encountered and re-encountered murals along the corridor, and have my favorites.

Sauntering down State Street one breezy summer day, I paused at a stoplight. Looming over the Gap store across the street and staring back at me from the side of a building, stretching several stories high, was the **Muddy Waters Tribute** (17 N. State St.). Muddy's face looks

Muddy Waters Tribute by Eduardo Kobra

pensive, as he holds his guitar like he's about to let out a piercing lick. I felt like the father of Chicago blues was watching over the city, and I was moved to tears. Painted in vibrant blocks of color, the mural had the hallmarks of one of my favorite artists, Brazilian-born-and-bred Eduardo Kobra.

It turns out Kobra is just one of many notable artists who have contributed to the Wabash Arts Corridor. Another is Never 2501, an Italian artist famous for murals intended to interact with viewers in interesting ways. His geometric, 8100-foot mural, **Almost Full** (59 E. Van Buren St.), covers an art deco building overlooking a parking garage. Black and white shapes cascade over a maroon backdrop, commanding attention and almost appearing to be an extension of the structure, due to a clever use of lines that creates a 3D effect.

From Bloom to Doom (1006 S. Michigan Ave.) by Dutch artist Collin van der Sluijs shows two endangered Illinois birds—the yellow-headed blackbird and red-headed woodpecker—surrounded by branches of spiraling native flowers on the side of a building. Until recently, it was easy to view by walking between buildings—but a 74-story condo is going up that will

From Bloom to Doom by Collin van der Sluijs

completely block the mural. That's the reality of a living urban canvas; some of the art is erased by demolished structures or new facades, and new pieces are introduced in other spaces. But you'll still be able to glimpse this artwork by slipping into the alley between the buildings, or from a window of the new building.

An interactive map of the Wabash Arts Corridor can be found on the website, but a casual walk reveals many of the murals, and part of the fun is the surprise of coming upon them on your own. Served by a number of L train lines, **Roosevelt station is a convenient starting point.** You'll be greeted almost immediately by ***Don't Fret*** (1152 S. Wabash Ave.), by the artist of the same name, featuring imagery conjuring college debt woes. Walk north up Wabash until you hit Van Buren Street, and then loop back south on either State or Michigan to catch a high concentration of murals. For an in-depth look as well as to learn about the artists and history, take the 1.5-hour **walking tour** (623 S. Wabash Ave., summer-fall, $18 adults, $12 students and seniors, free for children 5 and under) sponsored by Columbia College Chicago.

Connect with . . .
- **6** Groove to the Chicago blues
- **14** Get out to Grant Park
- **25** See world-class Impressionist art at the Art Institute of Chicago

29 Laugh out loud at Second City

Chi-Town Essential • Arts and Culture

Why Go: See a live show by the group that started a worldwide comedy revolution.

Where: 1616 N. Wells St. • 312/337-3992 • www.secondcity.com • $49-110 • L train Brown or Purple Lines to Sedgwick

Timing: Buy tickets online at least a month in advance for Mainstage shows and a few days in advance for the UP Comedy Club. Seating is general admission, and doors open 45 minutes before the show. Shows typically last about two hours.

Spawning celebrity alumni left and right, the Second City has become a comedic empire and brand of its own, so many people forget that the term "Second City" actually refers to Chicago—because its population used to be the second largest in the country after New York. In 1952, snarky *New Yorker* writer A. J. Liebling used the term as the title for a book deriding Chicago. The Second City founders decided to use this self-mocking name, and it's been a synonym for Chicago ever since. The improv school has famously served as training grounds for performers from Dan Aykroyd, John Belushi, and Gilda Radner—all of whom went on to become part of the original 1975 cast of *Saturday Night Live*—to Eugene Levy and Catherine O'Hara of TV series *Schitt's Creek* and Christopher Guest-directed mockumentaries like *Best in Show*. The Second City may now have global reach, with improv schools and comedy theater outposts in L.A. and Toronto, but the phenomenon started out in a tiny Old Town space in 1959.

The concept of theater games—the foundation of improv—was developed in Chicago by social worker and actor Viola Spolin. During the 1930s, she created a series of games to help children and recent immigrants communicate and work collaboratively. She taught these games to her actor son, Paul Sills, who put those techniques to use when he co-founded the Second City in 1959. He also brought in his mom to teach workshops to the ensemble's members. The comedy troupe quickly expanded and moved to a larger space. It's been operating out of its current home in Old Town since 1967.

The Second City's bustling multistory complex encompasses several stages, training center classrooms, and a restaurant, the 1959 Kitchen & Bar; I like to arrive before the show to have a meal here (you can eat during the shows, but it can be challenging on the small cabaret-style tables in the theaters). Live shows here always stir excitement. First-timers should see an improv show, but there are also revues that link thematically connected sketches as well as touring titles from other Second City locations. The schedule changes frequently, and it's a good idea to buy a ticket as soon as you see something that grabs your interest. Any of the shows all but guarantee sharp social observations and zany humor. Headlining shows are on the **Mainstage,** but my favorite Second City shows have been in the complex's **UP Comedy Club,** which features stand-up comedy as well as improv. The performers in this space feel a little freer, the shows are more personalized, and the cast is generally more diverse. If you sit close to the stage, you will be asked for skit suggestions and the results are usually undefeated.

▲ Second City performance

30 Learn about leather

Leather Archives & Museum

Museums • Arts and Culture

Why Go: Visit the only museum in the country dedicated to chronicling leather, BDSM, kink, and fetish culture.

Where: 6418 N. Greenview Ave. • 773/761-9200 • http://leatherarchives.org • 18 and over only • $10 • L train Red Line to Loyola • CTA bus #155 to Devon & Greenview

Timing: You can browse through the museum's exhibits in about an hour, but make an appointment and plan on several hours if you want to explore the archives.

There's not much to indicate the uniqueness of what's inside the unassuming rectangular brick building at the western edge of Rogers Park, other than huge white letters spelling out "LA & M"—although an LGBTQ pride flag hanging from a circular rail at the top of the stairs leading to the building's entrance and, above it, a handmade Black Lives Matter sign, hints at its inclusivity. LA & M stands for Leather Archives & Museum. It's the only museum in the country dedicated to preserving the history of and furthering education on alternative sex culture. It's easy to be impressed by the museum's equipment and artifacts—yes, that includes whips, harnesses, and handcuffs—but that's the tip of the iceberg in this deep dive into the overlooked leather, BDSM (bondage and discipline, dominance and submission), and fetish community.

The Leather Archives & Museum began as a repository for items left behind by members of the community who lost their lives to the AIDS epidemic in the 1980s. What started as a collection that was occasionally displayed for the public developed into this expansive museum and research facility for fetish history. Opened in 1991, the museum today features a mix of permanent and temporary exhibits. Spanning 10,000 square feet, it includes two floors, eight galleries, and an auditorium. Flags representing various fetish communities hang inside the museum.

Gay leather culture grew out of biker culture in the late 1940s, the hyper-masculine aesthetic a reaction to stereotypes about gay male appearances. The first gallery you'll enter in the

▲ fetish community flags

▲ bootblack accessories

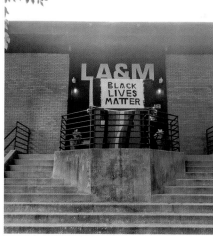

▲ Leather Archives & Museum entrance

▲ a display of leather paraphernalia

museum is filled with leather paraphernalia including jackets, hats, and vests from bars, clubs, and contests around the world and gives them context.

One of the museum's co-founders, the late activist and entrepreneur Chuck Renslow, opened the first gay leather bar in the United States in Chicago in 1958. The now-closed Gold Coast bar's walls were adorned with nude male erotica paintings by a longtime personal and professional partner of his, the late Dom "Etienne" Orejudos, a pioneer in his depiction of gay men in the leather community. His art also covers the museum's hallways. Renslow also established the International Mr. Leather conference and contest, held annually in Chicago since 1979—it grew out of a Gold Coast event. Photos of contest winners line several walls in the LA & M.

Downstairs is a dungeon, or play space, a common feature at BDSM clubs, parties, and events. Painted black and dimly lit, it features a collection of items including handcuffs, a straitjacket, and a bright red "spanking bench." There are also displays of accessories like muzzles and whips, accompanied by historical and functional details about each piece, as well as chains and straps with information on bondage safety precautions. The bootblack community, a niche within leather culture that involves passionate care of leather items, is represented with a bootblack stand, accompanied by brushes, boots, and a video.

The museum's library contains the real treasures, with books and magazines that center various sexual communities as well as videos documenting interviews with members of those communities. The archives contain 12,000 items, including graphic novels, art, scholarly publications, and novels; these are viewable by appointment.

Connect with . . .

① Wander the world in Rogers Park

31 Find peace at Garden of the Phoenix

Get Outside • Arts and Culture

Why Go: This Japanese garden is a magical oasis of calm in the middle of the city.

Where: S. Stony Island at Midway Plaisance/Cornell Dr. in Jackson Park • 773/256-0903 • www.chicagoparkdistrict.com • CTA bus #2 or #6 to 5800 S. Stony Island

Timing: Allow 1-2 hours to stroll and soak up the tranquility at this small but lovely garden. It's pleasant year-round, but at its prime in spring during its cherry blossom bloom.

Tucked in the northeastern corner of Wooded Island, behind Jackson Park's famous Museum of Science and Industry, the hidden gem that is **Garden of the Phoenix** feels like another world. I found it for the first time on a late summer's day after visiting the museum with a date. We roamed the Japanese garden's paths and sat on the rocks. Years later, I returned with my young kids and took photos of them sprawled on top of those same rocks.

The site, on Lake Michigan's shore east of the Hyde Park neighborhood, was once a swampland. Daniel Burnham and Frederick Law Olmsted (the designer of Central Park) transformed the area into an artificial island, surrounded by lagoons, as part of the 1893 World's Columbian Exposition. The Japanese government constructed the Ho-o-den, or Phoenix Temple—a recreation of an 11th-century Buddhist temple—to showcase Japan's history and culture to the World Fair's visitors. It was gifted to Chicago as a symbol of friendship and respect between the countries. The pavilion was a hit at the fair and inspired Frank Lloyd Wright to employ a Japanese aesthetic throughout his career.

Also called the **Osaka Garden** in honor of Chicago's sister city in Japan, the green space today greets visitors at its entrance with ***Skylanding,*** Yoko Ono's first public artwork in the United States, unveiled in 2016. Its metal petals sprout from the grass and soar toward the sky, representing Ono's focus on peace and contemplation. Inside the park, cherry trees line a gently lapping lagoon that winds through the green space. A short walk across zigzagging step-

Garden of the Phoenix

ping-stones leads you to the pavilion, with a raised platform that hosts Japanese tea ceremonies and other cultural displays. Lanterns carved out of rock line a stone pathway that wraps around ponds and a gently tumbling waterfall. A moon bridge spans the water amid the manicured trees and plants, and the neoclassical columns of the Museum of Science and Industry rise in the background. Strolling Hyde Parkers and photo shoots are common on the strikingly beautiful grounds, but it's rarely crowded here, and the serenity is palpable; most of the time, the only sounds you'll hear are birds chirping and water flowing.

It's not surprising that the best time to visit is in spring during **cherry blossom season,** when the garden glows with the snowy, fragrant flowers. The peak blooming period is brief, just 6-10 days, usually in late April or early May. This is also when you can expect crowds. It helps to check with the Chicago Park District (www.chicagoparkdistrict.com) for updates. But it's lovely to stroll through the garden year-round. It takes on an elegant stillness in winter that's especially stunning if there's snow. Just remember to bundle up, because gusts from the lake cut right through the grounds.

▲ a path winding through the garden

More World's Fair Sites

The Garden of the Phoenix is one of a few remaining vestiges of the 1893 World's Fair. The grand, pearl-colored buildings that made up the fairgrounds earned it the nickname "white city." The **Museum of Science and Industry** is housed in one of the original World's Fair structures, constructed as its Palace of Fine Arts. The 19th-century Beaux-Arts structure features grand columns, a copper dome, and Roman temple-style steps. Just south of the Garden of the Phoenix, at the intersection of Hayes Drive and Richards Drive, is the gleaming *Statue of the Republic,* which rises 24 feet above the street. Hyde Parkers sometimes call her "Big Mary," the name fair attendees gave the original statue, which was 100 feet tall and designed by Daniel Chester French (who also sculpted the Lincoln Memorial). This replica was erected in 1918 to commemorate the 25th anniversary of the World's Fair. To learn more about the city's World's Fair history, the Chicago Architecture Center's **White City Revisited tour** (312/922-8687, www.architecture.org/tours, $26) is an informative, two-hour experience.

Connect with . . .

🅛 Hang out in happening Hyde Park

㉑ Eat your way down 53rd Street

㉗ Catch the views from Promontory Point

32 Scoop up sweet treats

Food and Drink • Family Fun

Why Go: Indulge your sweet tooth at a destination-worthy ice cream parlor, candy shop, and bakery.

Where: Citywide

Timing: Budget 30-45 minutes in each shop if you plan on eating in.

I take my sweets seriously. I'm one of those people who avoids restaurants without good dessert menus. Sometimes I even eat dessert as a main course. And a simple chocolate bar or an ice cream cone doesn't do it for me; I need interesting flavors and unusual mixtures, so I've scouted out the best spots for well-made sweet treats.

Candy-striped awnings and a banana-yellow sign announce **Margie's Candies** (1960 N. Western Ave., 773-/384-1035) in Bucktown. A long glass case filled with handmade chocolates, vinyl booths with little jukeboxes on the tables, and an old cash register give vintage vibes—and in fact, this is the oldest candy shop in Chicago. Margie's opened in 1921, and it's been serving up heaping portions of ice cream and candies on doilies and silver trays ever since. Another shop is in North Center, but this is the original. Lines snake down the block to get into this small shop/ice cream parlor during summer, Valentine's Day, and most weekends, so come on a weekday afternoon so you can scoot into a booth and partake in an essential Chicago experience. Margie's is famous for its raspberry fudge sundae and world's largest terrapin (turtle) sundae (15 scoops!). I usually order the hot caramel sundae—and the pineapple pecan chicken salad, to balance the richness. Fair warning: Even a regular two-scoop sundae here contains a vat of ice cream in a clamshell, with a gravy boat of sauce on the side. Come equipped with your Chicago-worthy appetite.

Located in the Little Village neighborhood, home to a large Mexican American community, is **Dulcelandia** (3253 W. 26th St., 773/522-3816, http://dulcelandia.com)—the largest distributor of Mexican candies and piñatas in the Midwest. While there are a handful of locations

▲ stacks of Mexican candy at Dulcelandia

caramel sundae at Margie's Candies

Brown Sugar Bakery

Margie's Candies

around the city, this is the flagship store, and the largest. Simply walking into the sugar-scented shop—with its walls stacked full of colorful treats and piñatas of every shape and likeness hanging from the ceilings—is an eye-popping experience that stirs joy. Visitors are typically greeted with samples. Dulcelandia offers more than 1,000 candies representing every Mexican state, including classics like *ate de membrillo,* a sweet quince paste from Michoácan; *zapotitos,* fruit-shaped marzipan-like sweets made from pumpkin and dusted with cinnamon; and, my favorite, *paleta de cajeta,* a rich caramel lollipop made from goat's milk. I also love the mango and tamarind pops dusted in chili powder. There's a yogurt bar where you can add your own toppings, and a snack bar serving *elote* (grilled corn), nachos, and cookies. A crayon-colored seating area guarantees that you'll end up spending hours in this candyland.

Chatham's **Brown Sugar Bakery** (328 E. 75th St., 773/224-6262, www.brownsugarbakerychicago.com) will taunt your willpower; I have never managed to leave the bakery with just one or two treats like a reasonable person, and judging from the stacks of boxes carried out by other customers, I know I'm not alone. On a busy section of 75th Street, across from the likewise beloved Lem's Bar-B-Q, Brown Sugar Bakery is famous across the South Side for its grandma-worthy baked goods. The peach cobbler, sweet potato pie, and pineapple upside-down cake are all popular picks, but the caramel cake—featuring perfect layers of moist, yellow cake slathered in thick, buttery caramel—is, hands down, the greatest of all time. It's a hot commodity, so call in your order ahead of time if you want a whole cake. The shop is warmly run by owner Stephanie, who greets regulars by name and with a smile. She was also nominated for a James Beard Award for Outstanding Baker in 2019. Portions are generous and you can sample the dozens of desserts. Several tables and chairs let you savor your selections, though I've never seen anybody sitting at them; better to gorge yourself with piles of cakes and pies in private.

33 Appreciate Chicago's Black roots

DuSable Museum of African American History

Black Chicago • Museums

Why Go: Discover the vital history of Black Chicago and how it's influenced the nation.

Where: 740 E. 56th Pl. • 773/947-0600 • www.dusablemuseum.org • $12.50-14.50 adults, $9-11 students and seniors, $4-5 children 6-11, free for children 5 and under, free for all on Tues. • L train Red or Green Line to Garfield and then CTA bus #55 to 55th St. & Cottage Grove

Timing: Plan to spend about two hours here to take in the permanent as well as special exhibits.

The very name of the DuSable Museum of African American History encapsulates the significance and struggles of the Black citizens of Chicago. The city was founded by Jean Baptiste Point DuSable, a trilingual Black pioneer trader who was born in Haiti, educated in France, and in 1779 developed, with his Potawatomi wife, Kitihawa, the prosperous trading post that would become Chicago—a fact rarely taught in schools. A **bust of DuSable** (4 River Esplanade) marks the location of the trading post near the Chicago River, but there are still no full monuments to him. In 1987, Mayor Harold Washington dedicated a site along the lakefront, just east of the bust, as **DuSable Park** (401 N. Lake Shore Dr.); but more than 30 years later, park funding and plans have been ignored in favor of other sites.

Thankfully, we have the **DuSable Museum of African American History.** Founded in 1961 by legendary local artist and historian Margaret Burroughs along with a small group of educators and activists, the museum was created to give visibility to the Black history and culture that is too often ignored or overlooked. Housed in a 19th-century building perched on the expansive grounds of Washington Park, the museum greets visitors with beautifully intricate mosaics depicting DuSable's founders, as well as portraits of Jean Baptiste Point DuSable and Harold Washington, in the main lobby. The museum has six galleries laid out across two floors and an attached wing.

▲ exterior of the DuSable Museum

▲ interior of the DuSable Museum

▲ the DuSable Museum lobby

A South Side Powerhouse: Margaret Burroughs

Often called the first lady of African American Art, Dr. Margaret Burroughs has left a formidable legacy in Chicago. In addition to co-founding the DuSable Museum, she also co-founded the South Side Community Art Center, years earlier, at the age of 22. Dr. Burroughs also established an impressive career as a visual artist, earning acclaim as a printmaker using linoleum block prints, some of which are part of the Art Institute of Chicago's collection. She was also a writer and poet, producing children's books and several volumes of poetry, including the seminal *What Shall I Tell My Children Who Are Black?* As an educator, she taught at DuSable High School for over 20 years and was a Professor of Humanities at Kennedy-King College. But for all of her accomplishments, Dr. Burroughs was most noted for her capacity for encouraging and building pride in Black youth. I had the privilege of interviewing her for the school paper when I was in grad school. She peered at me, her signature beret cocked to the side of her head, and asked me how I planned to help my community when I graduated. I promised her that I would write about the African American artists that she helped nurture. And I have ever since.

The museum focuses on a mix of local and national history. Temporary exhibits dive deeply into Chicago people and events that left an impact nationally, such as *South Side Stories: The Art and Influence of Dr. Margaret T. Burroughs, 1960-1980* and *Troubled Waters: Chicago 1919 Race Riot*. It has four permanent exhibits, including **The Harold Washington Story,** which charts the journey of Chicago's first African American mayor, and, my favorite, **Freedom, Resistance, and the Journey Toward Equality,** which explores 400 years of the African American experience, covering the transatlantic slave trade, Jim Crow South, Great Migration, Civil Rights Movement, Harold Washington's election, and Barack Obama's election as Illinois senator and eventually the country's first Black president. Tracing the triumphs and pains of our non-stop battle for the recognition of our humanity, the multidimensional exhibit can be heart-wrenching. You can walk through a replica of the hold of a slave ship; touch fountains designated for Black and white people; hold a hat worn by a Pullman train porter (one of the few positions that allowed African Americans to join the middle class during segregation); and examine the bullet holes in the door of the Black Panthers' Chicago headquarters.

Other standouts among the large collection's 13,000 pieces include pioneering journalist and early Civil Rights leader Ida B. Wells' desk, works by historian and activist W. E. B. Du Bois, poetry by Langston Hughes, and drawings and prints by master artists Romare Bearden and Henry O. Tanner.

The DuSable also acts as headquarters for many beloved community events, including the **DuSable Museum Arts & Crafts Festival, Sounds of History Jazz Series,** and **Movies in the Park.** This free programming attracts diehards from all over the city who meet up with friends as an annual tradition at these family-friendly celebrations. The atmosphere is always festive and welcoming, with strangers welcomed as part of the larger community.

Connect with . . .

17 Hang out in happening Hyde Park

21 Eat your way down 53rd Street

34 See a play (or two) at the historic Biograph Theater

Arts and Culture

Why Go: Watch a production by one of two (or both!) theater companies in a landmark building with gangster history.

Where: 2433 N. Lincoln Ave. • 773/871-3000 • http://victorygardens.org • Victory Gardens tickets $30-65, resident theater company tickets $20-30 • L train Brown, Purple, or Red Lines to Fullerton

Timing: Victory Gardens productions typically run Wednesday-Sunday, with evening performances and additional matinees on weekends. Most shows last 1.5-2 hours.

The **Biograph Theater** opened in 1914 as a grand cinema. Listed on the National Register of Historic Places and an official Chicago Landmark, it has a free-standing ticket booth and an elegant canopy marquee topped with white terra-cotta that's stylistically striking amid the surrounding boutiques and cafés on a busy Lincoln Park block. It also occupies a significant place in Chicago gangster lore. In 1934, then "Public Enemy No. 1," John Dillinger, was shot by the FBI in an alley next to the theater after watching a movie. Dillinger, who led the country's most notorious bank robberies and jailbreaks, had undergone plastic surgery so that he could slip past lawmakers and enjoy a film, *Manhattan Melodrama,* with his two girlfriends—one of whom tipped off the FBI.

In 2004, **Victory Gardens** bought the theater. Its name is inscribed in innocuous script above the more prominent "Biograph," but the theater company otherwise retained the historic facade while renovating the interior into a state-of-the-art facility. Founded in 1974, Victory Gardens is a cultural jewel that produces acclaimed, thought-provoking theater focused on new works, which it presents on the mainstage. With a focus on social impact and inclusion, its shows draw a diverse audience spanning ages, genders, and ethnicities. It typically offers five productions a year, producing critically acclaimed plays like *Pipeline,* which examines the inequities of the nation's public school system and a teacher's determination to give her son more

Biograph Theater

than its poor offerings, and *Indecent,* which follows the true story of a Jewish playwright's 1923 Broadway production about a lesbian romance that outraged and intrigued audiences.

But what makes Victory Gardens truly special is that it also hosts a **Resident Theater Program** that affords other companies a physical home—its more intimate studio theater—over the course of multiple years, to grow their audiences. Companies have ranged from Teatro Vista, a beloved ensemble that produces stories about the multicultural Latinx experience, to Definition Theatre, a diverse company focused on socially relevant plays from underrepresented communities.

Come on a weekend to catch a matinee and an evening show to take advantage of the theatrical bounty. One day I treated myself to a double bill including *Tiny Beautiful Things,* a riveting production by Victory Gardens based on Cheryl Strayed's book about her time as beloved advice columnist "Sugar " and, later the same day, the Slideshow Theatre Company's *X,* a clever sci-fi thriller about a crew of researchers stranded on Pluto as an environmental apocalypse overtakes Earth.

35 Enjoy greens with a side of soul food in Garfield Park

Food and Drink • Family Fun

Why Go: A visit to one of the largest plant conservatories in the country can easily be combined with destination-worthy soul food nearby.

Where: Garfield Park neighborhood • L train Green Line to Conservatory-Central Park Dr. (Garfield Park Conservatory) and Laramie (MacArthur's)

Timing: A trip to the Garfield Park Conservatory and MacArthur's is always a treat, but especially enjoyable in winter, when the greenhouse's tropical temperatures combine perfectly with a comforting dose of soul food.

Plan on at least an hour in the conservatory and 20-40 minutes at MacArthur's. It takes just 10 minutes to drive from one to the other, so a ride-share is recommended if you're not in your own vehicle; otherwise, allow for 30-40 minutes by L train.

The **Garfield Park Conservatory** (300 W. Central Park Ave., 773/638-1766, http://garfield-conservatory.org, free) sits in the midst of a sprawling 184-acre stretch of green space. Opened in 1908 and listed on the National Register of Historic Places, the park is the signature landmark of the surrounding Garfield Park community on the West Side. It's often unfairly stereotyped as a "bad neighborhood." Yes, because of divestment and redlining, there is poverty and crime here, but not much around the park. East Garfield Park is lined with vintage buildings and wide boulevards that hint at the leisure playground that it was a century ago. It's changing again, thanks to its proximity to the Loop and affordable housing. There are recent signs of development—but hopefully no community displacement—with rehabbed homes, biking clubs, and The Hatchery food and beverage incubator nearby. The fact that one of the country's largest conservatories is located in a part of the city that visitors are discouraged from exploring makes it literally a hidden gem.

The conservatory was designed by landscape architect Jens Jensen in collaboration with Prairie School architects Schmidt, Garden & Martin, who gave the building a rounded shape that mimics the haystacks of the Midwest; the structure looks a bit like an inverted serving

▲ Garfield Park Conservatory

▲ a meal at MacArthur's Restaurant

▲ Palm House

▲ glass lily pad sculptures by Dale Chihuly in the koi pond at the Aroid House

dish. The conservatory's naturalistic display of varied flora—hailed as "landscape art under glass"—was considered groundbreaking for the era and remains visually compelling. Its greenhouse space covers two acres and includes the **Palm House,** boasting a 65-foot-high ceiling. This is where I spend the most time; the room showcases more than 70 types of palm trees and other tropical plants, and the ridged fan palms coupled with the conservatory's warm, moist air transport me to my favorite islands of Jamaica and St. Lucia. Other indoor spaces include the **Fern Room,** where the lush greenery surrounds a lagoon recalling the swampland that used to make up a large part of the city, and the **Aroid House,** notably home to anthuriums and a koi pond featuring yellow lily pad sculptures by celebrated glass artist Dale Chihuly. A couple of the rooms are more educational in nature, with the **Sugar From the Sun** room hosting themed botanical environments that demonstrate the process of photosynthesis, and the **Elizabeth Morse Genius Children's Gardens** offering interactive opportunities—to smell different flowers and herbs, or dig in the soil at special stations—for kids to learn about plants. The conservatory also has spectacular outdoor gardens, including the **Artist's Garden** (my favorite), featuring changing, creative displays of plants and showy flowers like dahlias that were loved by famous artists; the **Sensory Garden,** with beehives and a carnivorous bog; and the **Play & Grow Garden,** where kids can play with pebbles and mud.

While you're in the neighborhood, don't miss the opportunity to add on a meal at revered **MacArthur's Restaurant** (5412 W. Madison St., 773/261-2316, http://macarthursrestaurant. com), just 2.5 miles west of the park. Located on a corner of Madison Street, the West Side's main thoroughfare, the brick building stands like a monument to Chicago soul food. Amid the street's many businesses and churches, MacArthur's is always the most bustling; lines of people usually spill down the block. This family-owned restaurant has been a community hallmark since it opened in 1997. Locals know it as the spot with the best mac 'n' cheese and fried chicken on the West Side, but it's perhaps most famous as Barack Obama's favorite soul food joint. A framed photo of him, along with numerous other politicians and celebrities who have visited—Kanye West, Shaquille O'Neal, Alicia Keys, Bill Clinton, and Jesse Jackson, Jr.—cover the restaurant's walls. MacArthur's well-seasoned menu changes daily, but the cafeteria-style set up offers large portions of about 20 soul food staples on any given day, like fried catfish, smothered pork chops, black-eyed peas, collard greens, and candied yams. It's okay to ask about specials or the components of a particular dish, but don't expect a detailed narrative—the line moves fast. Slide your tray toward the cashier and don't skip the banana pudding. Most weekends are packed in general, but Sunday after 1pm is the busiest period, drawing in the after-church crowd. For a more leisurely, old-school experience, go on a weekday afternoon, when you can relax in a plaid booth or on the back patio and sink happily into a food coma.

36 Amble along the elevated 606 trail

Get Outside • Family Fun

Why Go: Meander an old rail line turned greenway dotted with art and lofty city views.

Where: Western trailhead at 1805 N. Ridgeway Ave., eastern trailhead in Walsh Park at 1722 N. Ashland Ave., 12 access points along Bloomington Ave., spaced about every quarter-mile • www.the606.org • L train Blue Line to Western or Damen

Timing: The 606 is 2.7 miles long. Budget a leisurely two hours to walk the whole thing since it's usually busy with strollers, joggers, bikers, and skaters. Give yourself a whole afternoon if you want to spend more time at the parks, lookouts, and art installations along the way.

The first time I walked down **The 606,** the sun was shining and the late spring day surprisingly warm. Fellow locals strolled the trail with gaping mouths; we were all giddy to be walking above the city streets. Passing rooftops and skyscrapers on the L train is one thing, but walking right next to them is something else. I wandered along the trail, perched 17 feet above the sidewalks, feeling like Dorothy on the yellow brick road; every few blocks revealed something new. At one point I sat on the tail of a dragon statue made out of steel and recycled tires, just gazing out at rooftops. At another, I joined some kids on a playground, and caught my size-10 feet in a spider web maze.

Although The 606, officially called the **Bloomingdale Trail,** is a relatively recent addition to Chicago, the trail is deeply connected to the city's history. Shortly after the Great Chicago Fire in 1871, an efficient way to rebuild the city was required; as part of this effort, the Chicago & Pacific Railroad laid tracks in the middle of Bloomingdale Avenue on the northwest side of the city. Its Bloomingdale Line made it easy to transport goods from rail ports to the Chicago River. Located at street level, the line crossed through several intersections without guard rails, and trains on the route frequently maimed and killed people. After years of protests and demonstrations about its dangers, the Chicago City Council finally passed an ordinance

strolling The 606

biking The 606

requiring the railway to be elevated, a project that was completed in 1915. Nearby companies and factories used the line to ship goods, and the area developed into an industrial center until the rise of interstate shipping. Freight traffic on the Bloomingdale Line ended in 2001, and the rail line laid dormant.

The **Logan Square, Humboldt Park, Bucktown** and **Wicker Park** neighborhoods located beneath the line boomed into popular residential areas just as nature reclaimed the tracks, with trees, flowers, and animals popping up. Residents created an unofficial nature trail and strolled the Bloomingdale Line for over a decade before it was formally developed into The 606 and opened in 2015.

The 606 takes its name from the first three numbers of Chicago zip codes and combines all the things that make the city great: green spaces, public art, and innovative architecture. The elevated path gives aerial views over the neighborhoods below, with glimpses of 18th-century factories, and there's lush, leafy landscaping along the trail, which connects to five parks. Benches and patches of grass are available at every access point for resting. And art—including murals, sculptures, and installations—are woven in along the way.

I like to walk a two-mile stretch of The 606, starting in Bucktown at the ingeniously named **Park No. 567** (1801 N. Milwaukee Ave.). Big limestone boulders shaded by bushy trees line the small park, inviting visitors to linger before venturing on. Local artist Jeff Zimmerman's massive, colorful *ConAgra Mural* faces the green space. The portrait of neighborhood residents—ranging in age, ethnicity, and expression—is interspersed with dandelions and other ephemera, surrounding a star-shaped form floating above hands cupping soil, a symbol of the universe. From here I wander to the far western end of the trail, concluding at **Exelon Observatory** (1801. N. Ridgeway Ave.) in Logan Square. At sunset, the observatory offers some of the best views in the city. In spring and summer, Chicago Park District astronomer, Joe Guzman, hosts "star talks" at the observatory.

A downloadable map is available on The 606 website. To avoid crowds, early mornings around 7am or evenings around 6pm are your best bet. **Divvy bike-share docks** (www.divvybikes.com) are located at several access points along the trail if you feel like cycling. The 606 is wheelchair-accessible, but it's important to remember that it's narrow; about 10 feet wide, with a two-foot running track along it.

▲ Tony Passero's *CoyWolf Mural* at an entrance to The 606 trail

No food or restroom facilities are located along the trail, but recommended nearby options just off The 606 in the surrounding neighborhoods include Costa Rican restaurant **Irazu** (1865 N. Milwaukee Ave., 773/252-5687, www.irazuchicago.com), just north of Park No. 567; vegetarian eatery **Handlebar** (2311 W. North Ave., 773/384-9546, www.handlebarchicago.com) at the Western Avenue access point; and **Humboldt Haus Sandwich Bar** (2956 W. North Ave., 773/904-8083) at the Humboldt Park access point.

Connect with . . .
20 Celebrate Borinquén culture at the National Museum of Puerto Rican Arts & Culture

Chi-Town Essential • Black Chicago • Museums

Why Go: Walk around one of the first planned industrial communities in the country and learn about its place in labor and African American history.

Where: 11141 S. Cottage Grove Ave. • 773/468-9310 • www.nps.gov/pull • free admission to the grounds, $5 admission to the National A. Philip Randolph Porter Museum

Timing: Budget about two hours. Note that the National A. Philip Randolph Pullman Porter Museum is generally closed mid-December–March except by advance appointment.

I grew up a five-minute drive from Pullman. Yet, while I knew people in all the surrounding neighborhoods, I didn't know anyone who lived in that little community, which always seemed set apart. The 19th-century Queen Anne–influenced row houses lining the main drag of Cottage Grove looked like red-brick points in a dusty old crown. I would visit the town's Hotel Florence with my family for weekend brunch and remember feeling like the building belonged to some ancient era—that it only appeared when we entered and would slip back into the past as soon as we stepped off the wraparound veranda.

Once I was older, I learned about the significance of Pullman. By that time the neighborhood had emptied, with the homes that had been passed down through families now left unoccupied after their owners died. In 2015, when then-President Obama designated Pullman a national monument, I knew that the community would be renewed and the neighborhood's history would finally get its due.

George Pullman amassed a fortune by developing comfortable and elegant accommodations—in particular, sleeper cars—for cross-country railroad trips. The first Pullman sleeper car was constructed in 1864, and demand grew so much that by 1867 he founded the Pullman Palace Car Company. The massive workforce required to manufacture the cars inspired Pullman to found one of the first planned industrial communities in the U.S., just south of Chicago's then-borders. Established in 1880, the town was noted for its sophisticated architecture.

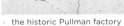
the historic Pullman factory

Pullman Clock Tower

row houses in the Pullman community

Pullman held rigid character expectations for anyone who lived in town—primarily white factory workers—and slashed wages when the economy faltered, without similarly cutting rents. In 1894, discontent workers organized a strike in Pullman factories, and were supported via boycott by the American Railway Union, to which many of them belonged. This devastated railway traffic across the country and marked a milestone in labor history as one of the first national labor disputes.

Another major milestone in the labor movement also arose out of Pullman. The company hired African Americans as porters, and became the largest employer of Black people in the country at the time. But African Americans were blocked from joining unions, so they had no say in their working conditions—such as putting in 400 hours a month. Led by A. Philip Randolph, the Pullman porters in 1925 formed the Brotherhood of Sleeping Car Porters, the country's first Black union. It took 12 years, but the union eventually signed a contract with the Pullman company to act as the bargaining agent for the Black workforce.

The Pullman company officially closed in 1969. Today, the area's historic houses are being snapped up by young families, and there's a fresh energy here. It's still small and tightknit, but feels like a community on the verge of becoming trendy.

Start an exploration of the national monument, which encompasses a total of 11 acres, in the Pullman Clock Tower building's **Shared Visitor Information Center** (11057 S. Cottage Grove Ave.). Orient yourself by watching the short video and viewing a model of the town, artifacts from Pullman cars, and displays about the factories. Then, grab a self-guided walking

▲ Hotel Florence

tour map or reserve a guided tour with a park ranger for a stroll around the grounds. Walk by the factory and historic row houses, then admire the grand exterior of the now-closed **Hotel Florence** (11114 S. Forrestville Ave.), an elaborate Queen Anne-style building that used to host railroad CEOs and other high society guests.

Next, visit the **National A. Philip Randolph Pullman Porter Museum** (10406 S. Maryland Ave., 773/850-8580, http://aprpullmanportermuseum.org, Apr.-mid-Dec.), which explores African American contributions to the country's labor history, with three floors of exhibits and artifacts, including oral histories of Pullman porters and a video about the Brotherhood of Sleeping Car Porters union. The museum offers an overview of both the local and national roles that the porters played in Civil Rights history.

38 Tune in to live local music

Arts and Culture

Why Go: Catch the excitement of a live Chicago band in one of the best music cities in the world.

Where: Citywide

Timing: At these bar-lounge venues, you can come just for a show or arrive early for drinks and stay late to hang out. All are general admission, standing room-only spaces, so arrive at least an hour and a half early if you want a seat.

As a music nerd who grew up to be a music writer, I've had the privilege of reviewing live music all over the world, so I can say—with only a slight bias—that Chicago surpasses most places in terms of the quality of its music scene. As the site of legendary blues, jazz, R&B, and gospel heritage, the city is also home to some of the best musicians in the world. There's nothing better than dancing to a dynamic local band on a balmy Chicago night.

The **Wild Hare & Singing Armadillo Frog Sanctuary** (2610 N. Halsted St., 773/770-3511, http://wildharemusic.com) has hosted the city's best local as well as international reggae artists, including Carl Brown & The Solid Gold Reggae Band, Morgan Heritage, Devon Brown, and Luciano. Formerly located in a cramped space amid the strip of bars in Wrigleyville—which still managed to transport you to bougainvillea-scented Jamaican nights with its high quality of live music—the venue relocated in 2012 to expanded digs in Lincoln Park. Its front bar is lined with wooden chairs that are always filled, so head for the black leather couches in the lounge, prime spots for drinking and eating before a show. An extensive dinner menu, with Jamaican mainstays like jerk chicken, oxtails, and mac 'n' cheese, really upgrades the experience; there's nothing like enjoying the island's spicy dishes while listening to reggae. I usually arrive hours before a show and stake out a spot near the stage for the best views. Admission is typically free during the week, and $5-10 on weekends. Ticket prices vary for touring acts, and it's best to purchase online in advance for these shows.

M Lounge

entrance of The Promontory

musicians performing at the Wild Hare & Singing Armadillo Frog Sanctuary

Although it's billed as a martini lounge, the South Loop's **M Lounge** (1520 S., Wabash Ave., 312/447-0201, www.mloungechicago.com) is a true neighborhood bar. I think of it as a South Side Cheers—except with style and music. A long, polished bar lined with bronze-colored stools serves as the main hub, with patrons drinking and chatting each other up. Locals love to hang out in the low-slung chairs and chocolate-colored loungers while DJs spin R&B and house tunes on weekends. On Tuesdays and Wednesdays, live jazz, blues, and R&B performers fill the space to standing room only. This is a popular first date spot because of the low-pressure atmosphere and tasteful music. Local performers who have played M Lounge include Delivery Point Band, Julia Huff & The Company Band, and DJ Ron Troupe. There's no cover charge for the shows, which further adds to the laid-back, living room vibe.

A brick hearth immediately grabs your attention as you step into **The Promontory** (5311 S. Lake Park Ave., 312/801-2100, www.promontorychicago.com). Inspired by the fire pit council rings of nearby namesake, Promontory Point, it casts a warm, stylish glow. This Hyde Park venue showcases a range of genres including blues, house, R&B, jazz, trap, and Afrobeat. The

⏶ DJ Jay Illa at The Promontory

crowd here is cool and fly, with lots of locals who love the eclectic lineup of events. On the 1st floor, an upscale restaurant serves food and drink, and upstairs, live music awaits in an intimate space with excellent acoustics; one of my favorite memories here is enjoying a flavorful bowl of butternut squash ravioli, then climbing the stairs to hear legendary Chicago blues harmonica player Billy Branch blast the night away. Bistro tables are scattered near the rectangular stage and a bar provides drinks in the back. Dancing typically breaks out in front of the stage and along the walls. Because of the room's small size, shows routinely fill to capacity, so buy tickets in advance online.

39 Explore the Burnham Wildlife Corridor

Get Outside • Arts and Culture

Why Go: Immerse yourself in diverse habitats and find art installations at the largest stretch of nature along Chicago's lakefront.

Where: Along Lake Michigan from McCormick Pl. south to E. 47th St. • www.chicago-parkdistrict.com • CTA bus #47 to Lake Park for Burnham Nature Sanctuary

Timing: It's about 3.5 miles from the northern end of the corridor to the southern end via the Lakefront Trail, which takes just over 1 hour to walk, or 30 minutes to bike, without stops. Allow yourself the leisure of at least 2-4 hours.

Spring and summer are the best seasons for bird-watching, blooms, and butterflies.

The South Side hosts many hidden treasures, and one of the most multidimensionally beautiful is the **Burnham Wildlife Corridor,** part of the larger **Burnham Park.** Hugging the lakeshore on either side of Lake Shore Drive for 100 acres, this cultivated green space encompasses three ecosystems: prairie, savanna, and woodland, which provide diverse habitats for migratory birds and other wildlife like coyotes and eastern cottontail rabbits. No matter the zooming cars of LSD, a peaceful vibe flows throughout the corridor.

The park is divided into three main areas. **McCormick Bird Sanctuary** (McCormick Pl. and Lake Shore Dr.) is an ingenious habitat of wildflowers and grasses planted atop an underground parking garage that serves as resting grounds for thousands of migratory birds on their way between Canada and Central and South America. South of the bird sanctuary, **Burnham Centennial Prairie** features an open expanse of grasses and native plants. **Burnham Nature Sanctuary** (E. 47th St. and Lake Shore Dr.) hosts grasslands, woodlands, and a butterfly garden at the corridor's southern end.

I like to stroll or bike through one section of the corridor at a time so I can give it my full attention. **Divvy bike stations** (www.divvy.com) are conveniently located at points along the way. My favorite section is the woodlands that edge the Burnham Nature Sanctuary. Wandering in the low-density forest of cottonwood, white ash, oak, and maple trees, as well as shrubs,

▲ nature trail through Burnham Wildlife Corridor

▲ view from the Burnham Wildlife Corridor

▲ *Sankofa for the Earth* sculpture by Dorian Sylvain and Arlene Turner Crawford

ground plants, and clusters of purple Missouri ironweed and prairie phlox wildflowers—with butterflies and birds flitting between them in summer—feels otherworldly, like you're in a fairy-tale forest, rather than adjacent to a busy expressway and neighborhoods.

In addition to nature trails through the corridor's natural areas, there are five **"gathering spaces"**—art installations with seating areas to encourage reflections on nature and culture. The integration of these artworks into the environment are what initially drew me to the corridor. Locating the art strewn around the corridor's winding paths is like a treasure hunt, though there are markers to guide you along the way (or you can download a map online). ***Sankofa for the Earth,*** located along the 43rd Street pedestrian bridge near the Burnham Nature Sanctuary, is my favorite piece. On one side, a sparkling mixed-media bird featuring mosaics and paintings—eye-catching amid the grasses and trees surrounding it—turns its head back toward its tail feathers. On the other side of the installation, images of Black Chicago idols including artist Margaret Burroughs, poet Gwendolyn Brooks, singer Sam Cooke, and Emmett Till—the Chicago boy whose lynching in Mississippi spurred the Civil Rights movement—cover the surface in a collage that merges into the branches of a tree laying on the ground. "Sankofa," a term from Ghana, means looking to the past to ground your future. With those historic figures gazing back at me as I sit in the grass, I feel profoundly supported. It's as if their spirits have seeped into the earth below and are now helping sustains us, both literally and figuratively.

Connect with . . .

2 Bike the Lakefront Trail
3 Go gallery-hopping in Bronzeville
17 Hang out in happening Hyde Park

40 Appreciate Indigenous culture

American Indian Center

Museums • Arts and Culture

Why Go: Learn about the city's Native American history and connect to the living culture at this community center.

Where: 3401 W. Ainslie St. • 773/275-5871 • http://aicchicago.org • free • L train Brown Line to Kimball • CTA bus #82 to Kimball & Ainslie

Timing: Allow an hour to visit the center and walk through the garden, which is a 20-minute walk away. Check the schedule online for programs and events.

Native Americans gave this city its name: They called it Checagou—a word with various meanings, from "stinky" to "onions" and "leeks"—referring to the vegetables that used to grow wild along Chicago's shores. Dozens of tribes lived on the land that's now Chicago, and they created a sprawling network of trails, dating back to the 1600s, that are largely unacknowledged but served as blueprints for what would become some of the city's major streets.

During the mid-20th century, the Indian Relocation Act along with the termination of sovereign status for many groups—efforts designed to push Native Americans from their traditional homes to metropolitan areas to assimilate—drew thousands of Indigenous people from across the country to Chicago. The **American Indian Center** was founded in 1953 to address the needs of the growing community and is the oldest urban Native American center in the United States. Located in the Albany Park neighborhood, the center serves as the major cultural and community resource for the Chicago area's population of 65,000 American Indians—the third-largest urban Indian population in the U.S., representing 175 different groups.

The center is located in a former school, its walls covered with the flags representing the Indigenous nations it serves, and is open to everyone. It's home to the **AIC Gallery,** which hosts rotating temporary exhibits that focus on various aspects of Native American history and culture, from contemporary art to political protests such as Standing Rock. Recent exhibits at the center have included *Visions of Home: Celebrating the Art of Leonard Peltier,* showcasing

a powwow at the American Indian Center

powwow dancer

a quill-making workshop

American Indian Center opening event

the imprisoned Native American freedom fighter's vivid paintings, and *Reclaim: Indigenizing Colonized Spaces,* a photo collection by Native American photojournalist Adam Sings In The Timber, featuring American Indians wearing traditional regalia on urbanized ancestral land.

The American Indian Center also hosts programs and events, such as workshops led by celebrated Indigenous artists and performances by singers and drummers. A popular offering is its **archery lessons** ($25, 50 minutes), which attract people from all over the city. The **annual powwow** ($15 general public admission, first weekend in Oct.), one of the largest in the Midwest, is probably the center's most notable event, a celebration of Native American song, dance, arts, and culture, with representatives from nearly 500 Indigenous groups attending from across North America.

About a mile west of the center is the **First Nations Garden** (corner of N. Pulaski Rd. and W. Wilson Ave.), created by the American Indian Center in partnership with the Chi-Nations Youth Council, an advocacy group for the city's Indigenous youth. It features traditional native plants and structures, such as a wigwam and tepee for storytelling, and is intended as a place of healing for the community and a way for others to learn about the culture. Walking on this small plot of ground, with its sunflowers waving in the air, feels like a way of honoring and connecting to those who first cared for this land hundreds of years ago.

41 Taste sweet candy history

Food and Drink • Family Fun

Why Go: Enjoy some of the treats that contributed to the city's standing as the one-time candy capital of the world.

Where: Citywide

Timing: Each candy shop merits about 20-30 minutes. CTA bus #157 takes you practically door to door from Fannie May (Michigan & S. Water) to Ferrara Bakery (Ogden & Taylor), though it's a 45-minute ride. World's Finest is located farther outside of downtown and is best accessed by car.

Although it's a little-known fact now, Chicago used to be called the "candy capital of the world." In 1884, the National Confectioners Association was formed in the city, helping regulate candy-making standards in the United States and establishing Chicago as the headquarters of the industry. More than a thousand candy factories were located in the city at its peak, around the mid-20th century. Classics like Baby Ruth, Juicy Fruit, Cracker Jack, Butterfinger, Andes Candies, Milky Way, Snickers, and Turtles were all created here. The city's central location and position as a railroad hub allowed it to access essential candy-making ingredients such as cream and butter from Wisconsin, corn products from Illinois, and sugar beets from Michigan. Growth in candy production coincided with Prohibition; when the sale and manufacturing of alcohol became illegal, bars shut down and ice cream parlors and confectionary shops became the new places to socialize. The city's mom-and-pop shops expanded into big factories that supplied most of the country's candy for decades. But by the 1980s and 1990s, candy manufacturers were hit with consolidation and global competition, and began relocating to cheaper cities in the country and abroad.

Today, Chicago is home to about 100 candy companies and still considered a major candy producer; in fact, the National Confectioners Association continues to hold its annual Sweets & Snacks Expo candy convention in the city. Some of the major candy makers that Chicago still hosts are **M&M Mars** (2019 N. Oak Park Ave.) and **Tootsie Roll Industries** (7401 S. Cicero

a Fannie May candy display

Tootsie Rolls

Lemonheads and Red Hots on display in Ferrara Bakery

Ave.), which produce a large portion of the nation's most popular candies. The factories are no longer open for tours, but M&M Mars hands out legendary candy hauls on Halloween.

Much of the Loop benefits from the delicious chocolate scent that wafts through the air, courtesy of the **Blommer Chocolate Company** (600 W. Kinzie St.), a family-owned candy maker. It's operated since 1939 and is the largest chocolate ingredient supplier in North America. In 2020, the company closed the chocolate store next to the factory, but continues to manufacture its products here, so the aroma lives on.

Fannie May (343 N. Michigan Ave., 312/453-0010, www.fanniemay.com) is synonymous with Chicago chocolates. Boxes of decadent and rich Fannie May chocolate eggs and pastel-green Mint Meltaways were part of my family's Easter tradition when I was growing up. The first store was established in 1920 by H. Teller Archibald. The classic Pixies—a blend of chocolate, caramel, and pecans—were created in 1946 and continue to be the shop's best seller. Today, there are about 50 Fannie May shops scattered all around the city and suburbs. Drop into the Loop's flagship Michigan Avenue location to sample a large selection of sweet treats, including Mint Meltaways as well as Trinidads and Carmarsh.

On Little Italy's main drag of Taylor Street lies **Ferrara Bakery** (2210 W. Taylor St., 312/666-2200, www.ferrarabakery.com), a shop with green awnings and a brick facade. It may look unassuming, but this is where a Chicago candy empire began. Salvatore Ferrara opened this bakery, the neighborhood's first pastry and candy shop, in 1908. The wedding cakes and cannolis sold quickly, but the best sellers were the sugar-coated almonds—known as Jordan almonds—that made for popular Italian wedding favors. Eventually, the bakery expanded into Ferrara Pan Candy Company (now the Ferrara Candy Company), and introduced Red Hots, Atomic Fireballs, Chuckles, and Lemonheads. Today, the Ferrara factory in Forest Park pumps out thousands of candy classics—including candy canes, of which they are the country's largest producer—while the bakery is famous for its cannolis and cannoli cake. The factory is no longer open for tours, but you can stop in for lunch and stock up on some sweets at the bakery. Although the interior has been updated, the vibe here remains old-school, with sunny yellow walls and an attentive owner.

Located in the manufacturing community of Archer Heights southwest of downtown, **World's Finest Chocolate** (4319 S. Pulaski Rd., 773/254-4762, http://worldsfinestchoco-

Ferrara Bakery

late.com) has been crafting from the cocoa bean since 1939. In 1949, it created a fundraising arm, supplying thousands of grade- and high-schoolers with tasty ways to raise money. World's Finest is famous for rich chocolate bars—some studded with almonds, some filled with rice crisps—but also sells chocolate mints and caramels. The outlet store, located next to the factory, offers premium chocolate at discounted prices, as well as factory seconds.

42 Pick up the signal
Museum of Broadcast Communications

Museums • Arts and Culture • Family Fun

Why Go: Delve into Chicago's rich radio and TV history at this hidden gem of a museum.

Where: 360 N. State St. • 312/245-8200 • http://museum.tv • $12-15 • L train Red Line to Grand or Brown, Orange, Purple, Green, or Pink Lines to State/Lake • CTA bus #3, #146, or #151 bus to Michigan & Hubbard

Timing: Expect to spend 1.5-2 hours browsing the exhibits. Add on more time to search the radio and TV show archives.

Chicago boasts so many large, internationally acclaimed museums that the city's smaller museums often get overlooked. With television show memorabilia, thousands of archived radio and TV shows, and historic artifacts like the cameras used to broadcast the first televised presidential debate between Richard Nixon and John F. Kennedy—which was taped in Chicago—the rarely crowded Museum of Broadcast Communications is one of those smaller museums that deserves a visit.

Too few people realize that from the 1920s to the mid-1950s, Chicago—not New York or Los Angeles—was a major broadcasting center. By the late 1920s, the city was a national radio production center. Shows like *Amos 'n' Andy* and *Fibber McGee and Molly* established the sitcom format, and *Painted Dreams* pioneered the soap opera. During the 1940s, Chicago-produced TV programs became known as the "Chicago School" of television. Their guiding principle was to lean into the uniqueness of the new medium—rather than conventions from radio, theater, or film—developing a sense of intimacy with the audience and fostering spontaneity, an approach that would influence the entire industry. When the East and West Coasts lured the city's network television professionals away from the city in the 1950s, the Chicago broadcast industry shifted focus, producing influential children's shows and network news. By the 1970s and 1980s, Chicago had birthed the syndicated daytime talk show, with Phil Donahue inventing the format, Oprah Winfrey perfecting it, and Jerry Springer pushing it into controversy.

Museum of Broadcast Communications

exhibit on Oprah Winfrey and her Harpo Studios

a Bozo the Clown exhibit

Garfield Goose and Friends exhibit

You can explore this history and more at the Museum of Broadcast Communications. It focuses on Chicago as well national broadcast developments through permanent and temporary exhibits. The interactive Chicago Television Gallery is my favorite, transporting me to my five-year-old self, sitting in front of the TV and squealing in anticipation. Being so close to the artifacts that I saw onscreen everyday as a kid—like the costumes from WGN's *Bozo's Circus,* the doghouse for Cuddly Dudley from *Ray Rayner and His Friends,* and the epaulet-adorned uniform worn by host Frazier Thomas from *Garfield Goose and Friends*—and watching clips from the shows is the most light-hearted fun I've had in a museum. The Radio Hall of Fame features antique radios and artifacts from notable radio shows, and holds an annual award ceremony to honor new inductees that have contributed to the development of the medium. Special exhibits are curated to connect with current pop culture and have focused on shows like *Saturday Night Live* and topics including the relationship between rock music and television.

The museum's extensive archives, a wide-ranging collection of 10,000 television shows, 8,000 commercials, and 50,000 hours of radio programs, are worth a deep dive. Videos and audio can be viewed or listened to in booths or online.

Also don't miss the gift shop, which sells goodies like turntables, vintage TV and radio show posters, and books about TV and radio personalities.

Connect with . . .

18 Chow down on classic Chicago eats (Pizzeria Due)

24 Ramble the Riverwalk

41 Taste sweet candy history (Fannie May)

43 Explore the eclectic in Evanston

Get Out of Town • Arts and Culture • Museums

Why Go: Find unexpected attractions in this quirky lakefront suburb.

Where: 13 miles north of downtown via Lake Shore Dr./U.S. 41 • L train Purple Line to Davis

Timing: Spend a day wandering the town's sights.

Set along the shores of Lake Michigan and dotted with Victorian homes and landscaped boulevards, Evanston is a picturesque village that draws lots of attention. Home of Northwestern University and noted for its diversity and liberal political activism, it's the rare suburb with a hip reputation. Adding to its progressive renown, in 2021 Evanston became the first city in the United States to approve a reparations program for African Americans. The town's progressive politics and openness to different perspectives has created an environment that has spawned quite a few quirky sights.

A visit to Evanston invariably starts on the miles of scenic lakefront. One of the most recognizable of its landmarks is the historic **Grosse Point Lighthouse** (2601 Sheridan Rd., 847/328-6961, www.grossepointlighthouse.net). Looming over Lake Michigan and surrounded by lush gardens, it was built in 1873—after one of the worst maritime disasters on the Great Lakes. Ship traffic and thick smoke from nearby factories caused a passenger steamer to crash into a schooner, killing 300 people. The memory of this horrific event hovers over the site, casting a melancholy atmosphere when you take in the panoramic views of Northwestern University and downtown skyscrapers. Tours inside the lighthouse, which hosts a small maritime museum, are available in summer (June-Sept., $6, cash only). The grounds are open for wandering year-round.

South down Chicago Avenue are a couple of the suburb's most compelling attractions. The **American Toby Jug Museum** (910 Chicago Ave., 877/862-9687, www.tobyjugmuseum.com, free) must be seen to believed. It boasts the largest collection of Toby jugs—more than 8,000—

▲ American Toby Jug Museum

▲ Dave's Down to Earth Rock Shop

▲ Grosse Point Lighthouse

in the world, drawing visitors from around the globe. Never heard of a Toby jug? Neither had I until I walked the rows and rows on display here. Toby jugs date back to the 1760s, when they started showing up in pubs, and are thought to be based on the popular British drinking song of the time, "The Brown Jug." Originally molded in the form of a stout man puffing a pipe and holding a mug of ale, with his tricorn hat forming a spout, the mugs have evolved to represent likenesses of various animals, characters, and people. At this small museum you'll see Toby jugs in forms ranging from 17th-century cockatoos to Xena the Warrior Princess to Barack Obama. For extra fun, I recommend participating in the scavenger hunt offered upon entry. Just around the corner is another sublime oddity, **Dave's Down to Earth Rock Shop** (711 S. Main St., 847/866-7374, http://davesrockshop.com, free). Established in 1970, it may look like just a crystal shop. But, besides being filled with thousands of gemstones, minerals, and other geological wonders, it also has a basement museum bursting with ancient fossils that the husband-and-wife owners collected themselves on travels across the West and abroad. Fossil specimens in-

▲ garage painting by Teresa Parod

clude insects encased in amber, a wooly mammoth tooth, a complete cave bear skeleton from France, and dinosaurs from China.

Evanston also hosts several acclaimed art galleries. My favorite is the unconventional, open-air **Garage Door Gallery** (alleys in the 1400 block between Thayer St. and Isabella St. and Thayer St. and Park Pl., www.teresaparod.com, free), northwest of downtown. Local artist Teresa Parod painted a jewel-toned garden scene on her garage door after returning from a trip to Cuba, where she was inspired by artists who transformed humble spaces. Her neighbors quickly lined up for their own garage door paintings. Now there's an alley gallery running through several residential blocks. Stroll through and you'll view images including a galaxy of planets, zinnias, sunflowers, and a charming group of purple elephants.

For an out-of-the-ordinary spot to grab a bite while in Evanston, a visit to **Found Kitchen & Social House** (1621 Chicago Ave., 847/868-8945, www.foundkitchen.com) is essential. Located in the heart of downtown, the beloved eatery serves a "flexitarian" menu, featuring local and seasonal ingredients, with items that might include a cauliflower salad or a pot pie filled with lobster mushrooms and rutabaga. The setting has a groovy "Jackie O. meets The Beatles, in India" theme, with embroidered couches, hanging tapestries, and acid-colored, upholstered chairs.

44 Retrace Hemingway's footsteps in Oak Park

Get Out of Town • Arts and Culture • Museums

Why Go: Head to this leafy suburban village to gain insight into one of its famous sons.

Where: 10 miles west of the Loop via I-290 • L train Green Line to Oak Park

Timing: Although only a 20-minute drive from downtown, Oak Park feels worlds away and deserves a full afternoon to explore.

With Victorian houses painted in crayon colors and rolling, emerald lawns flanked by blooming trees, Oak Park is a picturesque small town. It's also famously the home of the world's largest collection of Frank Lloyd Wright-designed buildings. But, for me, the most defining Oak Park creative is Ernest Hemingway, one of my favorite writers. I was drawn to the town for the first time to visit the **Ernest Hemingway Birthplace Museum** (339 N. Oak Park Ave., 708/445-3071, www.hemingwaybirthplace.com, $18), located in the heart of what's been dubbed the **Hemingway District.** As a teen journalist, I felt an affinity for Hemingway's concise writing style and was fascinated by the drama of his life. Begin your tour of Hemingway's hometown here as well. The museum is located in the 19th-century Queen Anne house where the writer was born, and which has been restored to how it looked during Ernest's childhood. A guide will take you through the home, offering family anecdotes and history, on a tour that lasts just under an hour. After walking the wooden floors of this house where he lived with his parents and grandparents and examining artifacts, toys, report cards, as well as a photo of the young writer in a dress (it seems that his mother raised him and his older sister, Marcelline, as twins), you'll come away with a deeper sense of what made the brilliant but troubled writer tick.

A few blocks north of the museum is Hemingway's Prairie School-style boyhood home, where he lived until he was 17. It's also where his father committed suicide, a pattern that Ernest and six other members of his family would repeat. A **plaque** (600 N. Kenilworth Ave.) identifies the historical significance of this stucco house, though it's not open to the public. Just

▲ Ernest Hemingway Birthplace Museum

south down the street, you'll find the stately **First United Church** (848 Lake St., 708/386-5215, www.firstunitedoakpark.com), where Ernest was christened and sang in the choir when it was known as the First Congregational Church. Right next door is the **Oak Park Public Library** (834 Lake St., 708/383-8200, www.oppl.org), which true literary nerds won't want to miss; its Hemingway collection includes the Nobel Laureate's high school essays and letters, plus rare editions of his work. Call in advance to make a reservation to view the collection.

For a sense of Papa Hemingway's more famous pastimes of drinking and feasting, drop by **Hemmingway's Bistro** (211 N. Oak Park Ave., 708/524-0806, http://hemmingwaysbistro.com)—yes, spelled with two "m"s, for whatever reason—an elegant French restaurant that successfully channels the charm of Paris in the 1920s, when the writer moved to the city with his first wife and hung out with other "Lost Generation" artists like Gertrude Stein, Picasso, and Ezra Pound. The restaurant features classic dishes like coq au vin, has an extensive wine list, and hosts live jazz on weekends.

And because Hemingway, an avid hunter and fisher, loved nature, round out your trip at

▲ Oak Park Conservatory

Oak Park's Other Favorite Son: Frank Lloyd Wright

It's hard to ignore the presence of Frank Lloyd Wright when you're in Oak Park. His famous architecture is the village's calling card. Wright spent his early career living in Oak Park, and he designed over 20 homes for residents, incorporating the elements that would later define the Prairie School movement. The most famous structure is the **Frank Lloyd Wright Home and Studio** (951 Chicago Ave., tours $15-30), which the architect designed when he was just 22. Another notable building is **Unity Temple** (875 Lake St., tours $15-40), which stands in elegant, geometric splendor. It's a UNESCO World Heritage Site and considered the greatest public building of Wright's Prairie School era. Both sites are maintained by the **Frank Lloyd Wright Trust** (312/994-4000, www.flwright.org).

the **Oak Park Conservatory** (615 Garfield St., 708/725-2400, www.pdop.org, $5 suggested donation), about a mile and a half south. All the landscapes nicely echo his travels around the globe: The Tropical Room connects to the writer's love of Cuba, while the Mediterranean Room recalls his time in Italy during World War I, and the Desert Room his time in the Kenyan desert.

45 Walk in the woods at Morton Arboretum

Get Outside • Get Out of Town • Family Fun

Why Go: Wander through miles of majestic landscape that make you feel like you're in another country.

Where: 25 miles west of downtown Chicago via I-290/I-88 • 4100 Rte. 53 • Lisle, IL • 630/968-0074 • www.mortonarb.org • $15 adults, $10 children

Timing: The drive to the arboretum from downtown Chicago takes 45-60 minutes, so once you're here, settle in for the day. While a trip to the arboretum is worthwhile any time of year, it's particularly spectacular in late October, during fall foliage.

Chicago is home to numerous parks and nature preserves, but if you want to feel like you've traveled to another part of the world, head to the Morton Arboretum. For a day out, I pack a hat, scarf, snacks, and a book, just like when I board a plane. On the drive up, the arboretum at first glance looks like just another strip of land amid the suburban sprawl. But once you park in the lot, you'll start to catch glimpses of the gardens. Established in 1922, the Morton Arboretum is recognized as one of North America's most comprehensive collections of trees and shrubs, encompassing 17,000 acres, with areas devoted to oaks, beeches, and maples; honeysuckles, roses, and magnolias; and the flora of Appalachia, Europe, Korea, and China.

Grab a map from the **visitors center;** it lays out the park's attractions—split into East and West Sides—as well as details what's blooming. The **Children's Garden** on the East Side and the **Sterling Pond/Lake Marmo** area on the West Side are popular. But I like to head for the quieter parts of the green space. When I arrive, I usually ask at the visitors center for recommendations.

Morton Arboretum offers various options for exploration. It has 9 miles of paved roads for scenic driving or biking. Biking is a pleasant way to experience the park, and rentals are seasonally available at the visitors center (May-Oct.), but my favorite way to enjoy the arboretum is on foot. There are 16 miles of pedestrian-only trails. Walking the paved path around **Meadow Lake,** right near the visitors center, is particularly soothing. But my favorite path is the **Heri-**

Lake Marmo

spring flowers

magnolias in bloom

The Morton Family Legacy

It took me years to realize that the classic table salt featuring the girl holding an umbrella in the rain while pouring out a canister of salt—which I never could make sense of as a kid—hails from the same family that founded the Morton Arboretum. Joy Morton founded the Morton Salt Company in 1885 in Chicago. Table salt stuck together in damp weather, so he developed an anti-clumping agent with magnesium-carbonate; this is where the slogan "when it rains it pours" comes from—an advertising campaign for Morton Salt intended to illuminate the product's innovation. Joy also grew up in a family interested in trees and horticulture; his dad, Julius Sterling Morton, founded Arbor Day in 1872—befitting the Morton family motto: "plant trees." Accordingly, Joy established a country estate in Lisle and started transforming it into the arboretum.

tage Trail, which starts at Parking Lot 13 on the East Side and leads you deep into the oak and maple woodlands. The trail spans 1.3 miles of paved and wood-chipped paths.

Every season at the arboretum holds its charms. In spring, it feels like a Japanese garden, with cherry trees blossoming and the heart-shaped leaves of *katsura* trees fluttering. In summer, it resembles an English meadow, with emerald swaths of grass and gardens brimming with pastel blooms. Autumn brings striking golden and crimson colors that form a vibrant halo over the arboretum; an open-air tram, the **Acorn Express** (schedule and fees vary), offers a guided tour of the tree collections, which is a fun way to take in the changing colors. And in winter, the evergreens and frozen ponds offer perfect holiday scenes. Popular seasonal festivals are also held in the arboretum, including the **Cider and Ale Festival** in fall and the **Illumination: Tree Lights** celebration in winter.

The arboretum has an on-site eatery, **Ginko Restaurant and Café,** for casual dining (think sandwiches and salads), but I recommend packing your own picnic to enjoy on the grounds.

46 Hike in Starved Rock State Park

Get Outside • Get Out of Town

Why Go: Wander trails through one of the state's most beautiful landscapes.

Where: 100 miles southwest of Chicago via I-55 and I-80 • 2678 E. 875th Rd., Oglesby, IL • 815/667-4726 • www2.illinois.gov •free

Timing: The park is a great natural escape from the city for a day or weekend. It takes about 1.5 hours to drive there from downtown.

Starved Rock State Park's namesake sandstone cliff is the most prominent natural landmark along the Illinois River. Its name comes from an Indigenous legend, referencing the 1760s assassination of Chief Pontiac of the Odawa people by a member of the Illiniwek group, and a subsequent battle for retribution. An Illiniwek band fled a retaliatory attack by climbing atop a 125-foot butte, and Odawa members and their Potawatomi allies surrounded the base of the rock, showering arrows at them and shattering the buckets they lowered to the river for water. Eventually, the Illiniwek members trapped on top of the rock died of starvation.

Starved Rock State Park became Illinois' first state park in 1911. It covers 2,630 acres and contains several different ecosystems: oak, maple, cedar, and pine forests; prairies; and wetlands. It's renowned for its 18 jaw-dropping sandstone canyons, formed by glacial meltwater and erosion over time. Every season at the park supplies a special treat. In spring and summer, the canyons glisten with waterfalls; in fall, the oak and maple forests turn deep crimson and gold; and in winter there are fewer hikers on the trails, the waterfalls transform into icefalls, and you might spot bald eagles soaring over the river—Plum Island, a 45-acre sanctuary in the middle of the Illinois River right across from the park, is a wintering spot for the birds.

Hiking some of the park's 13 miles of trails is the best way to take in the ancient beauty of this landscape. You can pick up a trail map and ask staff for recommendations at the **Starved Rock Visitor Center,** which also has exhibits on the park's flora and fauna, geology, and history. A 0.3-mile (one-way) trail from the visitors center takes you to the park's namesake rock

Starved Rock State Park

1: a pathway in the park **2:** camping at the park **3:** waterfall in LaSalle Canyon **4:** Council Overhang

Starved Rock's Sleepier Next-Door Neighbor

Just three miles southwest of Starved Rock State Park is **Matthiessen State Park** (2500 Rte. 78, 815/667-4868, www2.illinois.gov, free), which has five miles of hiking trails. It's overshadowed by its more famous neighbor, but is a good bet if you're looking for fewer crowds and similar scenery, with striking rock formations and waterfalls. Don't miss the 45-foot Cascade Falls.

formation; you can gaze up at it through towering oak and cottonwood trees. While the entire park possesses a serene majesty, the area around the cliff has a special energy. A popular hike, totaling just over four miles and moderate in difficulty, heads east along the river from the visitors center to **Sandstone Point Overlook** before heading inland on a spur to the **LaSalle Canyon,** then loops back to the visitors center through the woods. For a more peaceful hike, I like heading to the **Kaskaskia Canyon,** located at the quieter far eastern end of the park. It's an easy hike, about a mile round-trip, that includes a stunning waterfall—even more striking when it's frozen in winter—and wildflowers in spring and summer. The out-and-back trail starts at the parking lot for the Ottawa and Kaskaskia Canyon. On the way to Kaskaskia Canyon, you'll see the **Council Overhang,** an alcove carved into moss-covered rocks that was an important site to the Kaskaskia people.

If you want to make a weekend of it, **Starved Rock Lodge** (815/667-4211, www.starvedrocklodge.com), located right inside the park, offers rustic 1930s-era accommodations in its main building (there's also a modern wing) as well as cabins, and it has a restaurant with outdoor seating. Starved Rock State Park also has a year-round **campground** with more than 130 sites. Camping is extremely popular at the park, so book ahead.

For quality local eats, head to **Cajun Connection** (2958 N. Rte. 178, 816/667-9855, www.ronscajunconnection.com), three miles north of the park. Here you can grab an authentic taste of Louisiana; try the fried alligator, boudin balls, and crawfish étouffée.

47 Go back in time in Galena, Illinois

Get Out of Town • Museums • Get Outside

Why Go: This remarkably preserved riverfront town transports you to the 19th century.

Where: 165 miles northwest of Chicago via I-94 and U.S. 20

Timing: It takes about three hours to drive from Chicago to Galena. Expect to spend a relaxing weekend.

Illinois is filled with small towns, but few are as charming as Galena, located in the state's northwestern corner. Surrounded by rolling hills and green valleys, and with red-brick Victorian buildings set along the Galena River—a tributary of the Mississippi River—this port town is a visual delight. Most of its streets and structures look as they did during the town's 1860s heyday. Galena boasts more than 1,000 buildings listed on the National Register of Historic Places and is justifiably hailed as "an outdoor museum of the Victorian Midwest."

The small town is most noted for being the home of Ulysses S. Grant. In 1860, Grant moved to Galena with his family to work in his father's leather goods shop before departing soon after, in 1861, to serve in the Union Army during the Civil War. When he returned to Galena as a celebrated general in 1865, the town's residents presented him with a furnished Italianate mansion. Today you can tour the **Ulysses S. Grant Home** (500 Bouthillier St., 815/777-3310, www.granthome.org, $3-5), which is still filled with Grant's original furnishings and possessions, like his favorite green velvet chair and family bible. He only lived in the house briefly but returned to Galena for his 1868 presidential campaign, when the **Desoto House Hotel** (230 S. Main St., 815/777-0090, http://desotohouse.com) served as his headquarters; dating back to 1855, it's the oldest continuously operating hotel in the state. To learn more about the town's history, you can hop on a ride with **Galena Trolley Tours** (314 S. Main St., 815/777-1248, http://galenatrolleys.com, May-Oct.).

Simply strolling along the cobblestone sidewalks of Galena's **Main Street,** amusingly

▲ Galena Trolley Tours

▲ the Galena River

▲ Galena's Main Street

dubbed "Helluva Half Mile," is a pleasure, with its 125 quirky, independent businesses. **Root Beer Revelry** (228 S. Main St., 608/393-8283, www.rootbeerrevelry.com) serves dozens of root beer varieties on tap, in bottles, and over ice cream. **Great American Popcorn Company** (115 N. Main St., 815/777-4116, www.greatpopcorn.com) creates unusual flavors like Cherry Cheesecake and Hellfire & Damnation, a mix of habanero, cayenne, jalapeño, and other spices (free samples and over 250 flavors make it impossible to leave with just one bag). **Durty Gurt's** (235 N. Main St., 815/776-9990, www.durtygurtsburgerjoynt.com) is great for juicy burgers or, my favorite, the breaded grouper plate, and, especially, the boozy shakes; I always get the Very Berry with raspberry liqueur and strawberry ice cream.

Galena is also known for its vineyards, and there are several wineries around town. My pick is **Galena Cellars Vineyard & Winery** (4746 N. Ford Rd., 815/777-3235, http://galenacellars.com), family-owned for three generations. It has a tasting room on Main Street, but drive the 15 minutes west to its vineyards; the lush hillsides are the perfect backdrop for wine tastings.

▲ Ulysses S. Grant Home

To gain a greater sense of the area's natural beauty, go for a walk or bike ride along the **Galena River Trail** (www.cityofgalena.org), which winds for eight miles along the river, beginning just north of town and heading south to where it meets Mississippi River backwaters. Another good place to stretch your legs is just south of town, at the **Casper Bluff Land & Water Reserve** (870 S. Pilot Knob Rd., 815/858-9100, http://jdcf.org, free), which sits on Mississippi River bluffs and covers 85 acres that encompass 20 effigy mounds of the Ho-Chunk Nation. The Indigenous people's historic territory included parts of Illinois, Iowa, Minnesota, and Wisconsin. This effigy mound culture—raised piles of earth molded into the shapes of animals, symbols, humans, or plain conical figures and used for ceremonial and sometimes burial purpose—existed in Illinois and neighboring states primarily between AD 700-1000. Although the mounds are hard to spot, this is a scenic area to wander, with trails through the prairie and river views. Keep an eye out for bald eagles and other birds.

Part of what makes Galena such a great getaway is that it's brimming with historic inns, cottages, and B&Bs. My favorite is **Cloran Mansion Bed & Breakfast** (1237 Franklin St., 815/777-0583, http://cloranmansion.com), just north of downtown. The mansion embodies 19th-century elegance, and its landscaped grounds include a lily pad-strewn pond and gazebo. A highlight of a stay here is the six-course gourmet breakfast; the cinnamon swirl pancakes haunt my dreams.

Hit the beach in St. Joseph, Michigan

Get Out of Town • Get Outside • Family Fun

Why Go: Bask by the lake in the charming "Riviera of the Midwest."

Where: 100 miles east of Chicago via I-90 and I-94

Timing: It takes about 1.5-2 hours to drive to St. Joseph from Chicago. A weekend is the perfect amount of time to enjoy its offerings. Summer and early fall are the best seasons for a visit; many venues close by late fall.

St. Joseph's is called the "Riviera of the Midwest." Perched on a bluff along Lake Michigan's shoreline and dotted with dune-filled beaches, it's my favorite Midwestern beach town. It may be based around the same lake as Chicago, but the waters here seem to sparkle in a way I've never seen in the big city. The surrounding countryside, dotted with orchards and vineyards, also lends charm. Like most beach towns, St. Joe's keeps a relaxed pace; this isn't the place to be in a hurry or focusing on checking off a to-do list. Attractions can get crowded quickly, and service is slow-paced, but the warmth and friendliness of the locals make up for that.

Beach-hopping is how I spend most of my time here. **Silver Beach** (101 Broad St., http://berriencounty.org, $15 parking fee for non-residents May-Sept.), where the St. Joseph River empties into Lake Michigan immediately west of downtown, is the prettiest and most famous, with a pristine stretch of golden sand and views of the scenic North Pier Lighthouse. This is *the* beach for sunbathing and hanging out. It typically gets crowded early, so arrive by 9am if you want a spot on the sand. One of the beach's attractions is the **Silver Beach Carousel** (269/932-1141, www.silverbeachcarousel.com), an exceptionally beautiful indoor carousel housed in a tiered glass building that looks like a giant wedding cake. It features unusual, hand-carved animals like a clownfish, sea otter, and sea serpent that delight both kids and adults; my favorites are the flamingo and peacock. Across from the carousel is the **Whirlpool Compass Fountain** (spring-fall), which shoots up jets of water, a perfect device to wash off sand.

Just north of Silver Beach, across from the St. Joseph River, **Tiscornia Park Beach** (80

Silver Beach Carousel

Whirlpool Compass Fountain

Silver Beach

Tiscornia Park Beach

Ridgeway St., www.michigan.org, $2-7 parking fee for non-residents on summer weekends) is quieter. It has a picnic pavilion and pier access to the lighthouse and is also popular with kite surfers. **Lions Park Beach** (south end of Lions Park Dr., $2-7 parking fee for non-residents on summer weekends), south of Silver Beach, is a smaller slice of sand good for lounging uninterrupted in the sun. It also has a playground.

After a day at the beach, head to quaint downtown St. Joe's, filled with one-of-a-kind restaurants and shops. Make a beeline for **Silver Beach Pizza** (410 Vine St., 269/983-4743, http://silverbeachpizza.com) for the town's best pies. Then browse shops like **Bound For Freedom** (404 State St., 269/769-3732, www.boundforfreedom.org), a fair-trade, social justice-spirited boutique with goods like "Love Your Neighbor" T-shirts and reusable glass water bottles. Next door, **Purely Michigan** (406 State St., 269/983-3300, http://purelymi.com) supplies state-themed cuteness in the form of cookie cutters shaped like lower and upper Michigan. Several **wineries** are also located in town, sourced from nearby vineyards.

Just south of downtown, with a serene setting on the river, is the must-try **Clementine's Too** (1235 Broad St., 269/983-0990, www.ohmydarling.com), serving signature onion rings on a wooden peg. Another few miles south of town is **Nye's Apple Barn & Farm** (3151 Niles Rd., 269/429-0596). Be sure to stop by if you visit during August or September to pick peaches or apples and buy Amish jams and pies.

I like to hole up at **The Boulevard Inn** (521 Lake Blvd., 269/983-0520, www.theboulevardinn.com) when I come to St. Joe's for a weekend. It's the perfect spot to relax and take in the panoramic lake views.

49 Indulge in brats and brews in Milwaukee, Wisconsin

Get Out of Town • Food and Drink

Why Go: Delight in the delicious perks of this Midwestern city's German heritage.

Where: 90 miles north of Chicago via I-94 • Amtrak's *Hiawatha* line to Intermodal Station in downtown Milwaukee

Timing: It takes about 1.5 hours to drive to Milwaukee from Chicago. Make a summer weekend of it.

A long history of rivalry exists between Chicago and Milwaukee, Wisconsin's largest city—especially with our sports teams—but it's a silly, unfair comparison, like a little sister trying to compete by wearing her big sister's ill-fitting shoes. Milwaukee has its own sensibilities, a bit slower paced and grittier, with a quirky German personality and burgeoning arts-friendliness and sophistication. Like Chicago, the city sits along Lake Michigan and was originally inhabited by Algonquin, Potawatomi, and Ojibwe people. French fur traders and missionaries established the area as a trading post in the late 18th century. Polish, Irish, and German immigrants poured into the city during the mid-19th century, the latter bringing their brewing and sausage-making traditions with them, heavily influencing the city's developing culture. Pabst Brewing Company was founded in 1844, Schlitz Brewing Company in 1849, and Miller Brewing Company in 1855. By the 1870s, these brewing giants started expanding beyond local and regional sales to national and international markets, making Milwaukee one of the largest brewing centers in the country and earning it the nickname "Brew City."

Start your visit to the city at the **Riverwalk** (http://milwaukeeriverwalkdistrict.com), a pedestrian pathway that runs alongside the Milwaukee River to near where it flows into Lake Michigan, totaling 3.7 miles. It cuts through downtown and is lined with public art, restaurants, and buildings ranging from red-brick landmarks to gleaming skyscrapers. Right along the Riverwalk, **Saint Kate-The Arts Hotel** (139 E. Kilbourn Ave., 414/276-8686, www.saintkatearts. com)—which also houses a live music venue, a theater, and five art galleries—is my pick for

▲ bratwurst sausages

▲ Milwaukee's Miller beer

▲ Milwaukee River

Get a Taste of Black Milwaukee

Milwaukee may be known for brats and brews, but it's also home to a diverse array of other options. The city's population is 40 percent African American, which has left its mark on the food culture. In walking distance of the Riverwalk is the historic Black neighborhood of **Bronzeville,** where you'll find **Jewels Caribbean Bar & Restaurant** (2230 N. Dr. Martin Luther King Jr. Dr., 414/585-0678, http://jewelscaribbean.com). It serves classic island dishes like curry shrimp and jerk chicken and hosts a weekend line-up of jazz, R&B, and reggae ($5 cover). Farther northwest is **Sherman Park,** home to the groundbreaking small business hub **Sherman Phoenix** (3536 W. Fond du Lac Ave., 262/228-6021, www.shermanphoenix.com), which opened in 2016 in response to community upheaval after a fatal police shooting in the neighborhood. This incubator for Black entrepreneurs hosts 27 tenants, including **Funky Fresh Spring Rolls** (414/732-1531), offering rolls with inventive ingredients like shrimp gumbo, and **Sauce & Spice Pizza** (414/210-4478), a family-owned pizzeria that provides personalized pies with cracker-thin crusts and expertly seasoned ingredients such as a signature jerk chicken.

stylish, centrally located lodgings. Just south of the hotel is a must-stop: the **_Bronze Fonz,_** a 5-foot-6-inch statue—the same height as Henry Winkler, who played the iconic character—that pays tribute to Arthur "Fonzie" Fonzarelli, the ultimate cool guy from 1970s/1980s-era sitcom _Happy Days,_ which was set in Milwaukee during the 1950s.

Across the river, you'll find a trio of treats in close succession. **Milwaukee Brat House** (1013 N. Old World 3rd St., 414/273-8709, http://downtown.milwaukeebrathouse.com) serves up what's considered the city's best bratwurst. Settle inside or in the beer garden and order cheese curds, the beer cheese soup, and brats to your heart's content—the eatery offers more than a dozen varieties, ranging from a classic German-style sausage with sauerkraut and onions to a jalapeño-popper mac 'n' cheese version. Or you can build your own brat. Brat House also offers Beyond Meat brats, so there's no escaping the food coma, even if you're vegetarian. Beers are served two at a time, German-style. Just north up the block is **Usinger's Famous Sausage** (1030 N. Old World 3rd St., 414/276-9100, www.usinger.com), founded in 1880; stock up on brats here before you head out of town. Try the smoked bratwurst with cheddar or the spicy Cajun bratwurst. Another essential stop is the **Wisconsin Cheese Mart** (1048 N. Old

World 3rd St., 888/482-7700, www.wisconsincheesemart.com), a couple of doors down, where you can buy creamy cheese curds in batches of 3-5 pounds.

If you continue farther north along the Riverwalk, you'll pass through the **Beerline B neighborhood,** where the city's beer history is evident in facilities lining the path, like the old Schlitz brewery, now an office campus named **Schlitz Park** (1555 N. Rivercenter Dr.). A 10-minute walk farther north brings you to the newer-school **Lakefront Brewery** (1872 N. Commerce St., 414/372-8800, http://lakefrontbrewery.com), open since 1987, offering craft beers ranging from IPAs to gluten-free varieties. Have a pint on the riverfront patio.

Head west of downtown for a couple of other noteworthy beer-related attractions. Explore a beer baron's home at the **Pabst Mansion** (2000 W. Wisconsin Ave., 414/931-0808, www.pabstmansion.com, $11-15). Constructed in 1892, the Renaissance Revival estate is on the National Register of Historic Places. You can opt for a guided or self-guided tour. And you can't leave town without going on a tour of **Miller Brewery** (4251 W. State St., 414/931-2337, www.millerbrewerytour.com, $10). Learn about the company's history and top it off with a cold one.

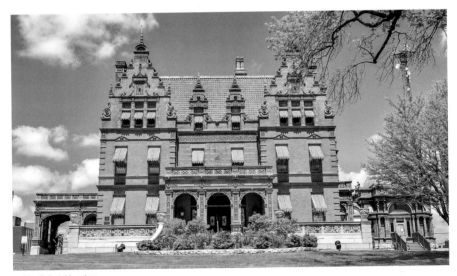

▲ the Pabst Mansion

50 Relax at Elkhart Lake, Wisconsin

Get Out of Town • Get Outside • Family Fun

Why Go: Unwind in this charming 19th century-era resort town with modern amenities and amusements.

Where: 150 miles north of Chicago via I-94

Timing: It takes about 2.5 hours to drive to Elkhart Lake, which is a great place for a weekend getaway in the summer. Many venues close outside the prime season (Memorial Day-Labor Day). Book at least a month in advance for hotels.

Sometimes there's nothing like leaving the fast pace of the big city and immersing yourself in the quiet of a small town. Elkhart Lake fits the bill. The pretty lakeside village has less than 1,000 residents and offers a singular vacation experience. Edging the shores of a pristine, sapphire blue lake—named by its original inhabitants, the Potawatomi, for its resemblance to an elk's heart—and enveloped by the canopy of the lush Kettle Moraine forest, the town is a dreamy retreat.

Thousands of springs feed the lake, which is revered not just for its beauty, but because it's believed to have curative powers. In 1886, the **Osthoff Resort** (101 Osthoff Ave., 855/876-3399, www.osthoff.com) opened to capitalize on the lake's rejuvenating qualities, and Elkhart Lake has been a popular Midwest resort town ever since. During the Gilded Age, Milwaukee beer barons and city folk from Chicago and St. Louis flocked to the town by rail for summer vacations. By the time Prohibition came around, it had developed into a gambler's haven, drawing gamers and gangsters looking for discreet hideaways. In the early 1950s, road races around the lake attracted racing fans, leading to the opening of the Road America facility that helped make the town a destination for professional race car drivers. Today, this historic resort town offers a range of wellness, adventure, and cultural activities, and its narrow streets are filled with smiling families roaming and perusing its Victorian shops.

Check in for the weekend at the Osthoff, or the more modern **Shore Club Wisconsin**

superbike racing at Road America

Off the Rail café

Elkhart Lake

(276 Victorian Village Dr., 920/876-3323, www.shoreclubwisconsin.com) for laid-back luxury, or **Christi's Inn** (121 S. East St., 920/876-3346, www.christisinn.com) for more modest lodgings.

After you're settled in, the first thing every visitor should do is get in, on, or near the lake. You can rent a pontoon, kayak, canoe, or paddleboard, but I love to hop a hydro bike and glide along the water. Water sport rentals are available at **Watersports on Elkhart Lake** (Shore Club Wisconsin lakefront, 920/377-0339, http://elkhartwatersports.com, May 30-Labor Day). Pedaling the sparkling waters, with views of the emerald foliage lining the lake, transports you to a slower-paced era.

The Osthoff Resort's **Aspira Spa** (920/876-5843, http://osthoff.com/aspira-spa) is a destination in itself. Treatments include the incorporation of lake waters and local cedar branches, and the setting's design is inspired by feng shui elements for ultimate serenity.

When you get hungry, head to **Off the Rail** (44 W. Gottfried St., 920/876-3655, www.offtherailelkhartlake.com), a popular café set in the town's historic railway depot, for hearty breakfast and lunch sandwiches. Have a seat on the patio, which is surrounded by tree-lined streets. For live music, scenic lake views, flatbreads, and cheese curds, go to the **Tiki Bar and Lounge** (open summer only) at the Shore Club Wisconsin, punctuated by bright blue umbrellas and drawing a slightly rowdy crowd.

Just outside of town are a couple of notable attractions. A stop by **Road America** (N7390 Hwy. 67, 800/365-7223, www.roadamerica.com, fees vary), south of town, is necessary. One of the world's fastest permanent road-racing tracks, Road America uses the natural topography of the area's rolling hills and ravines. The 640-acre motorsports complex has a four-mile track that hosts races but also allows public walking, biking, and disc golfing on specific summer evenings. It also offers Group Adventure Programs featuring activities like karting, geocaching, and off-roading. I tried my hand at relay racing a golf cart across an obstacle-strewn course, blindfolded, with just my partner's frantic directions to guide me; it was a memorable experience, to say the least.

North of town is **Henschel's Indian Museum and Trout Farm** (N8661 Holstein Rd., 920/876-3193, www.henschelsindianmuseumandtroutfarm.com, Memorial Day-Labor Day, $3-6), which has ancient effigy mounds that are not to be missed. The Henschel family has

▲ the author golf cart racing blindfolded at Road America

been farming this land since 1849—and uncovered numerous Native American artifacts while doing so, so many that Gary Henschel, part of the family's fifth generation, started an informal museum to display the findings, including arrowheads, tools, and animal skins. Visitors can also follow a trail through the woods on the property to see effigy mounds, raised formations of earth shaped like various animals and figures. The red ochre burial site is the oldest effigy mound in the state, dating to 600-800 BC.

51 Dine lakeside in Madison, Wisconsin

Get Out of Town • Food and Drink • Get Outside

Why Go: There's no better way to enjoy this vibrant city that's sandwiched between two lakes than by partaking in its waterfront food scene.

Where: 150 miles northwest of Chicago via I-90

Timing: It takes about 2.5 hours to drive to Madison. Spend a weekend in the summer.

Madison is mostly noted for being a college town—home as it is to the flagship University of Wisconsin campus—as well as the state capital, but it's also one of only two cities in the country built on an isthmus. Downtown is nestled between **Lake Mendota** to the west and **Lake Monona** to the east, lending this mid-sized Midwestern town a breezy urban oasis vibe. Madison is also an unexpected foodie destination with a thriving restaurant scene. The best way to enjoy this atypical town is to combine these two features.

Start a weekend trip by checking into **The Edgewater** (1001 Wisconsin Pl., 608/535-8200, www.theedgewater.com), a historic property perched on the shores of Lake Mendota in downtown. You can kick off your lakeside dining spree right away, with your pick of several stellar options right at the hotel. **The Boathouse** (http://boathousemadison.com) is The Edgewater's lake-level bistro, with dreamy waterfront views from the outdoor deck hugging the shore, as well as from inside via floor-to-ceiling windows. Order the lobster roll and a Mendota Colada. For locally sourced gourmet fare, head to **The Statehouse** (http://statehouse-madison.com). With dishes dubbed "modern Midwestern," the extensive menu features everything from fried cheese curds to a classic Wisconsin fish fry. The restaurant overlooks the lake from its perch on the hotel's 7th floor and also has a patio for warm-weather seating. In winter, rent a fire pit and enjoy frozen lake views and pizza at **The Icehouse** (www.icehousemadison.com), a seasonal pop-up. Get a good night's rest after your meal to prepare for an active day of dining and outdoor exploration tomorrow.

You'll need to occupy yourself somehow between meals. Since Madison is a serious biking

Lake Mendota

▲ Wisconsin State Capitol

▲ Olbrich Botanical Gardens

city, use its convenient bike-sharing system, **Madison BCycle** (http://madison.bcycle.com, $5 per 30 minutes, $15 day pass), to roll around. Glide down Wisconsin Avenue, around the imposing ivory marble buildings of the **Wisconsin State Capitol** (2 E. Main St.)—it's just a five-minute ride southeast—before heading northeast for about five miles and visiting the **Olbrich Botanical Gardens** (3300 Atwood Ave., 608/246-4550, www.olbrich.org, free), a waterfront beauty on Lake Monona, with 16 acres of outdoor gardens and manicured landscapes. Right next door, you can enjoy a beer and German specialties—maybe a snack like a soft pretzel or mini brats—at **The Biergarten at Olbrich Park** (3527 Atwood Ave., 608/237-3548, www.olbrichbiergarten.com, Apr.-Oct.), which has dazzling views of the lake and downtown skyline from its picnic tables spread out on the grass. Next, head back toward town to fill up on delicate thin-crust pizza and more Lake Monona vistas on the patio of the welcoming **Paisan's Restaurant** (131 W. Wilson St., 608/257-3832, www.paisansrest.com), established in 1950.

You could head back to The Edgewater or, if you have more energy to burn before dinner, explore a bonus lake. Bike a couple of miles west for the **University of Wisconsin-Madison Arboretum** (1207 Seminole Hwy., 608/263-7888, http://arboretum.wisc.edu, free). It has four miles of paved trails through various ecosystems, stretching along the shores of **Lake Wingra.**

For dinner, take a 20-minute drive counterclockwise around Lake Mendota from The Edgewater to arrive at **Mariner's Inn** (5339 Lighthouse Bay Dr., 608/246-3120, http://marinersmadison.com) for steaks, seafood, and sunset. Opened in 1966, the Madison classic has outdoor seating on a marina at the tip of Lake Mendota, where it meets the Yahara River that connects it with the city's other lakes. A classic supper club with nautical decor, the restaurant is decidedly old-school and offers both indoor and outdoor seating, both of which give exceptional views of the sun as it melts over the water and trees.

52 Enjoy the bounty of Door County, Wisconsin

Get Out of Town • Get Outside • Food and Drink

Why Go: From beaches and forests to orchards, vineyards, and culinary treats, this striking peninsula has it all.

Where: 235 miles north of Chicago via I-94 and I-43

Timing: It takes almost four hours to drive from Chicago to Sturgeon Bay, the closest and largest city in Door Country. Plan on a long weekend, at least.

If you've never traveled to Door County, Wisconsin, you've been missing out on the ultimate Midwest getaway. This stunning, pine-covered peninsula is your best bet for a nearby, year-round excursion. It's been called the "Cape Cod of the Midwest," with its 300 miles of shoreline and historic lighthouses. A narrow strip of land between Green Bay and Lake Michigan—only about 18 miles wide and 70 miles long—it's truly a natural paradise, featuring an unusual landscape of wetlands, forests, sand dunes, limestone slopes, sea caves, and outlying islands. Adding to the magic, Door County encompasses a number of delightful small towns offering their own charms. Sturgeon Bay is the peninsula's gateway town. But my favorites to base myself in are Fish Creek, Ephraim, and Sister Bay—all located in close proximity farther north along the peninsula's western side—which offer great restaurants, inns, and access to parks. **Highways 42** and **57** are the primary routes around the peninsula, and it takes about an hour to drive from one end to the other.

Fish Creek has vintage charm galore with its Victorian buildings and an exciting array of galleries and shops lining its Main Street. It's also the main access point for **Peninsula State Park** (9462 Shore Rd., 920/868-3258, http://dnr.wisconsin.go, $13 vehicle admission fee for non-residents), which has trails for hikers as well as some for bikers. The most striking is the two-mile **Eagle Trail,** which will give you a good taste of the peninsula's scenery. It loops through rocky terrain that takes you past Green Bay views and towering limestone cliffs, and through cedar forests filled with warblers, as well as thimbleberry and bellwort flowers. Bi-

▲ Door County

▲ cherry season

▲ Highway 42 in fall

cycling the stretch of Highway 42 that runs next to the park, from Egg Harbor in the south to Ephraim in the north, is also popular, especially during fall foliage season. Just south of town, you'll find **Lautenbach's Orchard Country Winery & Market** (9197 Hwy. 42, 920/868-3479, www.orchardcountry.com), offering beautiful scenes in spring and fall when its cherry and apple orchards, respectively, are in bloom. The farm also offers U-pick opportunities and wine tastings that include cherry riesling and cherry chardonnay. In winter, it offers sleigh rides, complete with prancing horses.

An absolute Door County requirement, no matter the season, is a traditional fish boil feast. This centuries-old tradition is a beloved part of the culture, brought over by Scandinavian settlers. The most famous fish boil is at Fish Creek's **White Gull Inn** (4225 Main St., 920/868-3517, www.whitegullinn.com); the master boiler oversees a big cauldron of whitefish and tosses kerosene onto the open fire when the fish oil rises to the top—resulting in leaping flames that cook the big chunks of fish and red potatoes quickly. The flavorful, tender fish is served with melted butter, lemon, and coleslaw. It takes skill to debone a whitefish, so servers actually come around and do it for you. A traditional end to the meal is a juicy slice of Door Country cherry pie. Fish boils take place on Wednesday and Friday-Sunday evenings May-October, and on Friday evenings the rest of the year. Reservations are a good idea.

Ephraim is the next town north from Fish Creek. This is where you'll find some of the region's best restaurants, including the stylish and locally sourced **Trixie's** (9996 Pioneer Ln., 902/854-8008, www.trixiesfoodandwine.com) and the casual waterfront **Chef's Hat** (3063 Church St., 920/854-2034, http://chefshatdoorcounty.com), serving high-quality comfort food. Ephraim is also home to **The Hardy Gallery** (3083 Anderson Ln., 920/854-2210, www.thehardy.org), which exhibits work by local and regional artists. Door County has a range of lodging choices, from campgrounds and cabins to B&Bs, condos, and resorts, but my favorite accommodations are in Ephraim. The **High Point Inn** (10386 Water St., 920/854-9773, www.highpointinn.com) has rooms featuring fireplaces and outdoor decks, and **Eagle Harbor Inn** (9914 Water St., 920/854-2121, www.eagleharborinn.com) offers elegant whirlpool suites, with the option to have breakfast baskets delivered to your room.

North of Ephraim, the town of **Sister Bay** is situated on the largest stretch of public waterfront in Door Country, with 1,900 feet of beautiful golden sand, as well as large grassy stretches, a gazebo, a stage, and a playground. The neighboring marina holds the annual **Marina Fest** (www.sisterbaymarina.com, Sat. before Labor Day), with fireworks, a water ski show, and live music.

Other popular activities in Door County include boating and fishing. Headquarters for these activities is in **Sturgeon Bay** at the **George K. Pinney County Park** (4879 Bay Shore Dr., www.co.door.wi.gov), which has a boat launch and plenty of perch and bass to catch. Other adventures to be had in Sturgeon Bay include zip-lining with **Door Country Adventure Center** (4497 Ploor Rd., 920/746-9539, www.dcadventurecenter.com). People tend to think of this as a warm-weather activity, but it offers a wintry thrill as well; I once tried it in the middle of a storm, and gliding across a field with the snow blowing in my face was invigorating. Sturgeon Bay is also host to the **Door County Wine Festival** (http://doorcountywinefest. com, June), at which you can taste offerings from local wineries. Or taste any time of year by following the **Door County Wine Trail** (www.doorcountywinetrail.com).

The **Door County Trolley** (8030 Hwy. 42, Egg Harbor, 920/868-1100, http://doorcountytrolley.com) offers recommended seasonal tours around the peninsula. The Spring Blossom Trolley Tour includes a carriage ride through scenic blooming areas, lunch, and a wine tasting, and the Lighthouse Tour takes you to some of Door county's 11 historic lighthouses.

INDEX

PHOTO CREDITS

All interior photos © Rosalind Cummings-Yeates except: title page photo: Tifonimages | Dreamstime.com; page 2 © (top to bottom) Antwon Mcmullen | Dreamstime.com; Candace Beckwith | Dreamstime.com; Shelly Bychowski | Dreamstime.com; Jimmy Lopes | Dreamstime.com; page 3 © (top to bottom) Bhofack2 | Dreamstime.com; Makeba Kedem Dubose; Francisco Blanco | Dreamstime.com; Rosalind Cummings-Yeates; page 4 © (top to bottom) Laura Iushewitz | Dreamstime.com; Russiangal | Dreamstime.com; Glenn Martin | Dreamstime.com; Jim Roberts | Dreamstime.com; page 5 © (top to bottom) Rosalind Cummings-Yeates; Joshua Resnick | Dreamstime.com; Sue Reddell; Laura Courteau | Dreamstime.com; page 11 © Shelly Bychowski | Dreamstime.com; page 12 © (top) Erik Lattwein | Dreamstime.com; page 13 © (top left) Ppy2010ha | Dreamstime.com; (top middle) Ranvestel Photographic / Choose Chicago; (top right) Adam Alexander Photography / Choose Chicago; page 14 © (top left) Juliscalzi | Dreamstime.com; (top right) Rawf88 | Dreamstime.com; page 15 © (top) Shelly Bychowski | Dreamstime.com; page 16 © (top left) Gallery Guichard; (top right) Black Ensemble Theater; page 17 © (top left) Nljpics | Dreamstime.com; (top right) Jim Roberts | Dreamstime.com; page 18 © (top) James Andrews | Dreamstime.com; page 19 © (top left) Gerald Marella | Dreamstime.com; (top right) Jason P Ross | Dreamstime.com; page 25 © (top left) Dawid Swierczek | Dreamstime.com; (top right) James Andrews | Dreamstime.com; (bottom) James Kirkikis | Dreamstime.com; page 26 © Dreamstime Agency | Dreamstime.com; page 29 © (top) Gallery Guichard; (bottom) Rohan Ayinde Smith; page 30 © Faie Afrikan Art Gallery; page 33 © (top right) David Danku; (bottom) David Danku; page 41 © (bottom) Candace Beckwith | Dreamstime.com; page 49 © REUTERS / Alamy Stock Photo; page 50 © REUTERS / Alamy Stock Photo; page 53 © Black Ensemble Theater; page 54 © Black Ensemble Theater; page 57 © Anderm | Dreamstime.com; page 58 © Shelly Bychowski | Dreamstime.com; page 61 © Jim Roberts | Dreamstime.com; page 62 © Jim Roberts | Dreamstime.com; page 65 © (top) David Danku; page 69 © (top left) Lightpainter | Dreamstime.com; (bottom) Toxawww | Dreamstime.com; page 70 © Lightpainter | Dreamstime.com; page 73 © (top left) Jim Roberts | Dreamstime.com; (top right) Sergii Figurnyi | Dreamstime.com; (bottom left) Ffooter | Dreamstime.com; (bottom right) James Byard | Dreamstime.com; page 75 © Dibrova | Dreamstime.com; page 77 © (top left) Artitwpd | Dreamstime.com; (top right) Bdingman | Dreamstime.com; (bottom left) James Andrews | Dreamstime.com; (bottom right) Floyd Webb; page 78 © Kimberly Lewis | Dreamstime.com; page 82 © Open Books; page 85 © (top) Christopher Andrew; (bottom) Ross Floyd; page 87 © Rosa Enrico Branch; page 89 © (top left) Bhofack2 | Dreamstime.com; (top right) Jim Roberts | Dreamstime.com; (bottom right) Jim Zielinski | Dreamstime.com; page 93 © Jon Bilous | Dreamstime.com; page 94 © Mohsin Khan | Dreamstime.com; page 97 © (top) NMPRAC; (bottom) NMPRAC; page 98 © NMPRAC; page 102 © (top) Virtue / Lindsey Becker

ACKNOWLEDGMENTS

First of all, I would like to thank my grandmother Charity, grandfather Joseph, great aunt Essie, and father, who all made the challenging Great Migration journey to Chicago so that I could grow up in this fascinating city and document its many experiences. I am grateful to my mother for providing childhood stories that would shape my understanding of Chicago history. I'd also like to thank my late grad-school chair, the legendary Charles-Gene McDaniel, who first showed me the significance of the printed word and the importance of accuracy. Special thanks to Jerry Glover, for going above and beyond to make sure that I had all the benefits and opportunities from this book.

Floyd Webb, thanks so much for sharing your unending tales of Chicago history and generous photography expertise. Thanks to David Danku for always being there and supplying photos when I couldn't get them myself. Makeba Kedem-Dubose, thank you for making sure that I had all the details on Chicago Black artists. Thanks to Dwana De La Cerna for helping me get the best candy pics. Mario Smith, thanks for sharing all of your Hyde Park wisdom. Many thanks to Sue Redell for her Madison insights and tea fortifications.

I am grateful to my editor, Kristi Mitsuda, for helping my words shine and making sure that alliteration is well-represented.